Edward Hull

Our Coal Resources at the Close of the nineteenth Century

Edward Hull

Our Coal Resources at the Close of the nineteenth Century

ISBN/EAN: 9783743330078

Manufactured in Europe, USA, Canada, Australia, Japa

Cover: Foto ©ninafisch / pixelio.de

Manufactured and distributed by brebook publishing software (www.brebook.com)

Edward Hull

Our Coal Resources at the Close of the nineteenth Century

CONTENTS.

CHAPTER I.

INTRODUCTORY 1

CHAPTER II.

CLASSIFICATION OF BRITISH COAL-FIELDS . . 26

CHAPTER III.

ENGLISH COAL-FIELDS.

MIDLAND GROUP:—
1. The North Staffordshire Coal-field 29
2. The South Staffordshire Coal-field 32
3. The Leicestershire Coal-field 34
4. The Warwickshire Coal-field 37

CHAPTER IV.

ENGLISH COAL-FIELDS—continued.

NORTH MIDLAND GROUP:—
1. The Yorkshire, Derbyshire and Nottinghamshire Coal-field 41

CHAPTER V.

ENGLISH COAL-FIELDS—continued.

THE GREAT NORTHERN COAL-FIELDS:—
1. Durham and Northumberland 45
2. Cumberland 48

CHAPTER VI.

ENGLISH COAL-FIELDS—continued.

	PAGE
THE NORTH-WESTERN GROUP :—	
1. Lancashire and East Cheshire	50
2. Coalbrook Dale	53
3. Forest of Wyre	55

CHAPTER VII.

ENGLISH COAL-FIELDS—continued.

WESTERN GROUP :—	
1. Bristol and Somersetshire Coal-basin	56
2. Forest of Dean, Gloucestershire	59

CHAPTER VIII.

THE WELSH COAL-FIELDS.

1. The South Wales Basin (including Monmouthshire)	62
2. Denbighshire Coal-field	68
3. Flintshire Coal-field	70

CHAPTER IX.

THE SCOTTISH COAL-FIELDS.

POSITION AND DIVISIONS :—	73
1. The Clyde Basin	74
2. The Midlothian and Haddington Coal-basin	75
3. The Fifeshire Coal-field	76
4. The Clackmannan Coal-field	76
5. The Ayrshire Coal-field	77
6. The Lesmahago Coal-basin	78
7. The Dumfries-shire Coal-basins	78
8. Resources of the Scottish Coal-fields	79

CHAPTER X.

COAL SOUTH OF THE THAMES 85

CHAPTER XI.

SUMMARY OF ESTIMATED RESOURCES OF THE BRITISH COAL-FIELDS AT THE CLOSE OF THE NINETEENTH CENTURY 90

CHAPTER XII.

BRITISH COAL RESOURCES.

1. Quantity of available coal under the Permian and Triassic formations 92
2. Summary of available amount of coal under the Permian and other overlying formations 99
3. Revised Estimates of Resources of Concealed Coal-fields . 100
4. Summary 103
5. Total estimated quantity of coal in the visible and concealed coal-fields, within a depth of 4000 feet, remaining at the close of the Nineteenth Century 105

CHAPTER XIII.

TABLE OF QUANTITY OF COAL RAISED IN THE DIFFERENT COAL-FIELDS DURING THE YEAR 1895 106

CHAPTER XIV.

APPROXIMATE LIMIT OF DEEP MINING . . 107

PHYSICAL IMPEDIMENTS:—1. Temperature of Mines; 2. Dukinfield Colliery; 3. Rose Bridge Colliery; 4. Cause of Difference in Rate of Increase of Temperature; 5. Mean Result; 6. Ventilation; 7. Temperature of Air-Current; 8. Effects of the Seasons; 9. Effect of Increased Circulation of Air-Current; 10. Effect of Humidity, or Dryness of the Air; 11. Effects of Pressure.

CHAPTER XV.

PROGRESSIVE AND RETROGRESSIVE MINING DISTRICTS 129

  1. Progressive Coal Areas; 2. Stationary Coal Areas; 3. Retrogressive Coal Areas 130

CHAPTER XVI.

FOREIGN COAL-FIELDS.

I. COUNTRIES NOT UNDER THE BRITISH CROWN:—
    1. The Russian Empire; 2. Sweden; 3. Germany; 4. Belgium; 5. France; 6. Spain; 7. Austria-Hungary; 8. Italy; 9. Japan; 10. United States . 133

II. COUNTRIES UNDER THE BRITISH CROWN:—
    1. British India; 2. Canada; 3. New South Wales; 4. Victoria; 5. Queensland; 6. Tasmania; 7. New Zealand; 8. Cape of Good Hope; 9. Natal . . 136

III. THE AVERAGE VALUE OF COAL AT THE PIT'S MOUTH IN VARIOUS COUNTRIES 138

IV. PERCENTAGE OF COAL CONSUMED IN VARIOUS COUNTRIES 140

CHAPTER XVII.

A FORECAST 141

APPENDICES.

I. OUTPUT OF COAL FROM THE COAL-FIELDS OF THE UNITED KINGDOM SINCE 1870 147

II. PRODUCTION OF COAL IN THE UNITED KINGDOM DURING THE YEAR 1896 148

III. COAL RESOURCES OF CONTINENTAL STATES . . . 150

IV. PRODUCTION OF BRITISH PIG-IRON IN 1896 . . . 152

INDEX 153

OUR COAL RESOURCES.

CHAPTER I.

INTRODUCTORY.

THE close of the Nineteenth Century seems a fitting occasion for taking stock of the coal-resources of the British Islands, upon which so much of the commercial prosperity of the Empire depends. A recent writer, when describing the powerful machinery lately brought into operation for generating electrical force by a small section of the Niagara Falls, says, that the question determining the future of a country, as regards its manufacturing resources, will not be, whether it contains large stores of coal, but whether it possesses water-power. Whatever amount of truth there may be in this statement, there can be no doubt that falling water is a more permanent source of power than coal; the latter being exhaustible, the former, perennial and recuperative. There is only one country, however, that possesses its Falls of Niagara, and it is certain that it is not

Great Britain. The numerous waterfalls and rapids to be found amongst our hills and valleys are comparatively small, both as regards height and volume; and although much greater use might be made of these for generating electrical energy than is the case at present, the advantages from them can only be trivial as compared with those derived from the combustion of the stores of mineral fuel contained in our coal-fields. For the present, and for centuries to come, we must depend on our coal-resources; and it is, therefore, of first importance that we should endeavour to ascertain, as far as the nature of the enquiry permits, the extent and durability of these resources.

The latter question was ably discussed by the late Professor Jevons in his well-known work entitled, 'The Coal Question,' published more than thirty years ago,[*] in which he has shown that every improvement for the economising of labour has resulted in an increased consumption of coal; and he contends that coal being the great source of power, and being required for every great extension of industry, the consumption of it must keep pace with the progress of population, and the extension of manufactures and industrial pursuits. Since the year in which Professor Jevons' work was published, an enormous expansion has taken place in the output of coal in Great Britain. At that period the output was a

[*] Published in 1865.

little over 98 million of tons*; it has now nearly doubled this quantity, and there can be little doubt that by the end of the century the quantity will fall little, if at all, short of 200 millions of tons per annum.

When in the year 1859 I estimated, in my work on 'The Coal-fields of Great Britain,' the quantity of available coal remaining in the British area, and within a vertical limit of 4000 feet in depth, at about 79,843 millions of tons, the result was considered reassuring, because at the then rate of production this would have sufficed to last for nearly a thousand years. This estimated quantity was exceeded by that of the Royal Coal Commission, presided over by the Duke of Argyll, published a few years afterwards.† But notwithstanding the ability with which the investigations of the Commissioners and their assistants was conducted, I have always held that for practical purposes their estimates were largely excessive; chiefly on the ground of the inclusion of seams of coal between one and two feet in thickness; seams which could never be worked at great depths or at a remunerative cost.‡ Another point, however, of much importance is the fact that within recent years, owing to the progress of mining, we are now better informed regarding the extent of our coal-

---

* According to 'The Mineral Statistics of Great Britain,' 98,150,587, including Ireland.   † Report, 1871.

‡ I have stated at some length elsewhere the cause of my objections to their results, 'Coal-Fields of Great Britain,' 4th ed., p. 506.

fields than we were when the Coal Commission reported, and these results have tended considerably to modify our views concerning the possible extension of beds of coal under the newer formations by which the visible coal-fields are surrounded; this is especially the case in regard to the extension of the midland Carboniferous strata, to which I shall have occasion to refer in a future page.

Limit of Depth for Coal-Mines.—As regards the limit of depth at which beds of coal can be worked, there is, of course, no definite certainty. I need only here observe that the cost of working, the expense of machinery and sinking of shafts, the superincumbent pressure of the overlying strata, and the degree of temperature—these are all increasing factors which have to be taken into account as we penetrate deeper and deeper into the solid crust. Down to a depth of three thousand feet, both temperature and pressure are capable of being kept within limits of health and safety; but beyond this depth they become very serious obstacles to coal-mining. At this depth, the natural temperature of the strata, where they are approximately horizontal, is nearly 100° Fahr., but by means of ventilation this temperature may be reduced considerably. The experiments carried out at Rose Bridge Colliery, near Wigan, at a depth of 1800 feet from the surface, show that by means of the air-current necessary for ventilating the mine, the temperature is reduced by amounts varying from 15° to 20°, according to the temperature of the intake air at the bottom of the shaft, and the distance through which the current has travelled.* The results determined by the Royal Commission on this subject are also reassuring,† and, as a general result, justify the expectation that seams of coal of good quality and sufficient thickness will be workable at depths down to 4000 feet below the surface.‡ But, great as is this depth, it is certain, on geological grounds, that there are seams of coal in South Wales, Somersetshire, Cheshire, and other districts in the north and centre of England which descend to much greater depths, and which, under the hypothesis of a 4000 feet limit, are beyond the reach of mining enterprise.

The practical limitation of depth being thus agreed upon, and the quantity of coal remaining in the British coal-fields down to this depth having been approximately determined at the close of the

---

* 'Coal-fields of Great Britain,' p. 497. All the temperatures here given are according to Fahrenheit scale.

† Report, vol. i. p. 82.

‡ This limit of depth has been adopted by the Commissioners, by Professor Jevons in his work 'The Coal Question,' and originally by myself as far back as the year 1859. There is, therefore, practical unanimity on this important point.

§ From geological considerations we have reason to believe that under the plain of Cheshire there are seams descending to depths of 7000 or 8000 feet, and the same statement holds true in the case of the South Wales coal-basin.

year 1879, I propose to bring the question of our resources in this mineral down to the close of the present century (1) by deducting the quantity which has been exploited since my last estimates in 1879 down to the returns for 1895, and (2) by deducting estimated quantities for the remaining four years for all the coal-fields of importance. For this we have the necessary data, owing to the systematic manner in which the returns of worked minerals are lcollected by the Secretary of State for the Home Department, through the agency of the Inspectors of Mines, and published in a tabulated form after the close of each successive year.* I have dealt with the question of temperature in deep mines further on.†

Causes conducive to Expansion in our Coal Production.—Amongst the many causes conducive to the expansion of our coal-production, the most important may be ranged under the following heads :—

1. The increase of population.

2. The increase of steam power in our Navy and mercantile marine.

3. The increase in our export of coal.

---

* The special department for collecting and publishing the 'Mineral Statistics' was formerly entrusted to the late Mr. Robert Hunt, F.R.S., Keeper of the Mining Records, but since his decease is carried on by Mr. James B. Jordan, of the Home Office, to whom I am indebted for much assistance in obtaining returns. The returns for 1896, which have just been received, amount to 195,351,951 tons. † *Vide* p. 111.

4. The increase in British manufactures and railways, both at home and in foreign countries.

It would be out of place for me to attempt to deal adequately with these important subjects; and only a few remarks upon them must suffice, as bearing upon the question of increase of our coal consumption.

1. As regards the increase of population, it was estimated by the late Mr. Robert Hunt that the consumption of coal by each individual might be taken at one ton per head per annum of the whole population. By the census of 1891, it was ascertained that the population of the United Kingdom, including islands, amounted to 37,821,209 souls, and if we allow for a decennial increase at the rate of ten per cent, the population will reach the enormous number of 41,603,329 at the beginning of the twentieth century. During the decennial period between 1881 and 1891 the increase of the population was for England and Wales at the rate of 11·65 per cent., for Scotland 7·76 per cent., but as regards Ireland there was an actual diminution at the rate of 9·08 per cent. On the whole, the rate of increase for the entire population of the United Kingdom since the year 1811 appears to have been with slight variation at a diminishing ratio; so that we are tolerably safe in assuming the rate for the present decennial period at 10 per cent., as above stated. If then we take Mr. Hunt's estimate as approxi-

mately accurate, this will dispose of over 41 millions of tons of coal for the domestic consumption of the population at the end of this century; being about one-fifth of the entire estimated output of coal at that time.

2. *Naval Steam Power.*—Ever since the year 1812, in which the *Comet* first began to ply on the Clyde between Glasgow and Greenock, a new demand on our coal resources has arisen. Steam power has completely replaced the sail in the Royal Navy, and only to a less extent in our merchant service. During the same period iron and steel have been gradually replacing wood in naval construction until the latter is only used for the building of small craft, coasters, and fishing fleets, and from this cause also an additional drain on our coal supplies has sprung up, of ever increasing amount; so that within the memory of many now living the "Wooden Walls of Old England" have been transformed into walls of iron and steel. But this is a subject which more properly comes under the 4th head; when we are dealing with the question of naval construction, we shall have occasion to revert to it again.

3. *Export of Coal.*—For naval purposes no country in the world produces better coal than that derived from the mines of South Wales and the north-east of England. This variety of coal, known as "steam-coal," is, therefore, in ever increasing

demand for the furnaces of our ships, which are supplied therewith not only at British ports but at coaling stations scattered all over the globe. The peculiar excellence of this class of coal for the generation of steam lies in the fact that the proportion of carbon is very large and the proportion of gas small; it occupies in fact a position between bituminous coal and anthracite.* Coaling stations supplied with British coal, especially that shipped from South Wales, are to be found in nearly all parts of the world, extending even to China, Japan, Australia, India, Ceylon, the Cape, Brazil, West Indian islands, Peru, Chili, and the islands of the Atlantic and Pacific. According to the returns prepared by order of the House of Commons no less than 31,756,368 tons were shipped from British ports for foreign countries and British settlements in 1894,† and in the following year the quantity was nearly the same; ‡ so that we export about one-sixth of our entire output to foreign parts, largely for the use of ships of the mercantile marine and of the Royal Navy. Notwithstanding the development of the coal-fields

---

* In anthracite the proportion of carbon varies from 90 to 92 per cent., in steam coal from 80 to 90, and in bituminous coal from 70 to 80. The heating power is proportionate to the amount of carbon; but where the proportion of gaseous matter is exceedingly small, as in pure anthracite, there is difficulty in keeping the fires alight, and the boiler tubes heated.

† Return by Mr. R. W. Hanbury, dated 31st August, 1895.

‡ 'Mineral Statistics' for 1895.

of foreign countries, which has been considerable during the last quarter of a century—especially in America, Borneo, Japan, and Australia—British coal, owing to its superior quality, still holds its own; and, notwithstanding the high price due to freightage, competes successfully with that of many countries possessing supplies of their own, for the use of ocean steamers.

4. *British Manufactures.*—The condition of the iron manufacturing industries has always exercised a most important influence on the production of coal; so that a large demand for iron draws with it a large demand for mineral fuel, both for smelting the ores and for manipulating the metal. Between the years 1860 and 1862 the production of iron ore in Great Britain and Ireland increased from about eight millions to eighteen millions of tons, producing about one-third of pig-iron. After the year 1882, however, there was a rapid decline, partly due to a falling off in the demand for railway-iron, and partly from the general substitution of steel rails for those made of rolled iron.* The general introduction of steel rails has been of great advantage to the railway companies; for, notwithstanding the additional cost of steel rails over those of rolled iron (now not very great), the former will last two or three times as long; and there is also the advantage that great expense in re-laying

---

* The falling off is also partly due to the vast growth of iron-production in Belgium and Germany.

the rails at short intervals, together with interruption in the traffic, is avoided.* England is enormously rich in ores of iron, especially of the earthy, or "basic," varieties which occur amongst the Liassic and Oolitic formations.† Notwithstanding this abundance of ore, however, these earthy varieties have to meet a heavy competition from foreign countries, especially from Spain, and large quantities are annually imported from that country for the furnaces of South Wales, the Tees, and the Clyde. In 1895, the quantity of pig-iron smelted in British furnaces amounted to 7,703,459 tons, for which 15,224,517 tons of coal or coke were used, which is approximately two tons of coal for every ton of iron.‡ It will thus be seen that an increase, or falling off, in the production of iron materially affects the demand for coal; and if we assume that an additional ton of coal is used for each ton of manufactured iron or steel, then each ton of the latter represents the consumption of three tons of coal.

* I am informed by C. J. Bowen Cooke, of the London and North-Western Railway, that some of the steel rails laid down on the main lines in 1876, just twenty years ago, are still so sound as not to require replacing; and that the average "life" of steel rails is seventeen or eighteen years, about twice that of iron rails.

† In the counties of Oxford, Northampton, Lincoln, and the Cleveland district of Yorkshire.

‡ 'Mineral Statistics' for 1895. Besides the basic varieties of ore there are the rich hæmatites of Cumberland and North Lancashire, the clay-band and black-band ores from the coal-measures, and the aluminous hæmatites of Co. Antrim in Ireland. For the production of pig-iron in 1896, see Appendix IV.

The vast expansion of the British Empire which has been in progress during the latter part of the century has necessarily exercised an important influence on our manufacturing industries. The demand for railways and steamships cannot but continue, and even increase, with the progress of civilisation in those countries over which England stretches her beneficent ægis. We may look forward with confidence to the extension of railway communication throughout Central and Southern Africa and the Valley of the Nile. Let us hope that the Uganda railroad is only a pioneer to many similar undertakings for opening up Central Africa in the near future; and it is gratifying to know that the demand for railway iron is already perceptibly felt.* It is very remarkable that British iron, whether in the form of "pig" or the manufactured article, is exported to all parts of the world, even including those of our colonies, such as British North America, which possess considerable supplies of their own.† In the year 1895 we exported to foreign countries 866,568 tons of pig-iron, 457,552 tons of railway iron, and 451,122 tons of various kinds of manufactured iron—in all 1,775,242 tons; and if we may be per-

---

* Speech by Mr. C. T. Ritchie, President of the Board of Trade, at Croydon, 25th November, 1896.

† 'Mineral Statistics' for 1895, p. 72. In the catalogue of countries to which iron is exported are included Australasia, Belgium, Brazil, British North America, British South Africa, Chili, Germany, Holland, Italy, Russia, Sweden, United States of America and other countries.

mitted to forestall the future, we may, from the returning signs of manufacturing activity, expect that the exports for 1896 will have been still larger.

The great increase which has taken place in the construction of ships in iron and steel within the last twenty years has contributed to the increased demand for iron, and, therefore, for coal. As late as 1875 the number of ships built of wood was considerable, amounting to 209, with a tonnage of 57,187 tons; but in 1895 the number had fallen to 23, with a total of only 2415 tons. In the former year also steel was not used for ship-building, but it has now almost superseded iron; for out of a total of 309 ships built of metal in 1895, only 27 were built of rolled iron plates, while the use of wood had almost disappeared in our building yards, or was only used for sailing ships and small craft. During the same period the average size of vessels built has also increased threefold; and the proportion of steam, to sailing, tonnage is twenty-five to one. And not only does Great Britain retain the lead of all countries in the building of ships, but she also builds ships for nearly all countries. Thus in the year 1894 out of a total of 614 ships launched, no fewer than 97 passed into the hands of foreign owners, while 517 remained with British owners.*

It is remarkable that the United States of America, with their enormous resources both in coal and iron, and numerous ports on the Atlantic sea-

* 'Lloyd's Register of British and Foreign Shipping,' 1894.

board, should still be far behind Great Britain in reference to the possession of a mercantile marine and in the construction of tonnage. But such is apparently the result of the protectionist policy adopted by the States, which has raised the prices of the materials of construction and increased the rate of wages to an extent which makes it impossible for them to compete with this country on advantageous terms in the construction of ships. As regards tonnage, it is remarkable that, for a number of years past, the total tonnage built within the United States has not exceeded 220,000 tons, or about one-fifth part of the tonnage built in the United Kingdom. This includes the tonnage built for the Great Lakes, which exceeds that built on the seaboard, or on the great rivers like the Delaware and Mississippi. At the utmost, the total tonnage of the United States does not exceed 4,703,880 tons at the present time; and of this no less than 3,600,000 tons, or more than 70 per cent. of the whole, is of timber, and driven by the sail.* The general effect of this state of things is to throw a large proportion of American shipping trade into British hands; and of this the following occurrence, which I have on reliable authority, will offer a good illustration :—

An American mercantile firm, desiring to have several large steamers built for trading purposes, made enquiries through a London firm, with a view

* *The Times*, 26th December, 1896.

of ascertaining the cost of construction. Tenders were offered by a firm of British ship-builders at 20,000*l*. for each vessel, and were duly forwarded to the American house. A reply was received that they were astonished at the moderate price proposed, as the cost of building the ships in America would be equivalent to 50,000*l*. each; but, that notwithstanding, they were unable to give the order for building, as they had found that American law prohibited Americans from owning any ships but those built in America itself, unless derelict on the United States coast. Could anything be better devised for throwing trade into British hands?

Her command of supplies of coal and iron, together with the facilities afforded by her numerous sea-ports, gives Great Britain advantages which few, if any other countries possess for this branch of industry; and so we find that all her principal centres for ship-building, namely, Barrow, the Clyde, the Mersey, the Tees, the Tyne, the Wear, and Belfast Lough, are situated under these conditions, with the honourable exception of Belfast, which in spite of the fact that both the coal and iron have to be imported from England or Scotland, takes a good position as a ship-building centre both as regards the size of the vessels and the quality of the work.* The

* In 1894 the Belfast yards turned out twenty-three steamers and one sailing vessel, with a total tonnage of 96,800 tons. It is satisfactory to see that the Thames is once again becoming a seat of the ship-building trade.

above figures do not include ships of war, many of which are built at the Admiralty dockyards, of which 31, with a displacement of 32,971 tons, were launched in the year 1894; and of these 29 were for the British Government. In 1896 provision was made by Parliament for the construction of five battle-ships of 12,500 tons each. Our ocean highways are now traversed by steamships of huge dimensions, yet such as science, combined with experience in naval construction and the requirements of the period, shows to be best fitted for combining safety with speed and large carrying capacity. Several of the Atlantic liners plying between Liverpool and New York register nearly 10,000 tons,* while the *China*, the largest of the ships belonging to the Peninsular and Oriental Company,† has a capacity of 8000 tons, and three additional ships of similar dimensions, and of 11,000 horse-power are almost ready for active service.‡ But large as is the tonnage of many of our passenger ships, it is surpassed by that of the battle-ships of the Royal Navy with a displacement ranging from 10 to 15,000 tons, such as the *Majestic*, the *Royal Sovereign*, and the *Nile*.§

* The Cunard Liner *Campania* reaches a gross tonnage of 12,950 tons, the *Majestic* and *Teutonic* 9965 tons each, and the *Etruria* 8100 tons, all of these being Atlantic liners.
† Generally known as the P. and O. Company.
‡ Fifty-sixth Annual Report, 1896.
§ 'United Service Mag.,' Dec. 1896.

The returns issued at the commencement of 1897 through Lloyd's Register of ship-building during the previous year afford a timely confirmation of the above statements, regarding the progress of this branch of trade and manufacture. Exclusive of ships of war, 696 vessels, of 1,159,751 tons gross, were launched from ports in the United Kingdom. There were also 55 ships of war launched at Government and private yards, having a total displacement of nearly 164,000 tons. The total was therefore rather more than 1,323,000 tons, exceeding that of 1895 by more than 208,000 tons. This increase is due mainly to steam tonnage, which reached a higher figure than in any previous year; and of the whole number of ships about 99 per cent. were built of steel; wrought iron having been almost entirely superseded.

I refer to these details in order to bring before the mind of the reader the magnitude of the demand which the building and fitting out of iron ships of all classes must have on the supply of iron in the first instance, and of coal for its reduction from the ore and subsequent conversion into the manufactured article, in the second.

Proportion of Coal consumed per Head of Population.—In referring to the estimate of one ton per head of the population, as suggested by Mr. Robert Hunt, it was only understood as applicable to the personal, or domestic, consumption. If we estimate the consumption per head as including every kind of use, whether for fuel or for manufactures and motive-power, the resulting proportion will be necessarily materially increased. The subject has been placed before us in a very clear manner in the tables published with the 'Mineral Statistics' for 1895, which range from the year 1873 downwards to the year of publication.*

From this table we gather that after deducting the quantity of coal exported in each year, either in the form of solid coal or patent fuel and coke, the proportion of coal remaining per head of the population amounted to 3·75 tons for the year 1895. This proportion does not appear to have very materially varied within the period of twenty-two years comprehended by the table, except when abnormal causes tending to the disturbance of trade and manufactures arose, as was the case in the year 1893, when there occurred the great strike and lock-out in the Midland districts. In this year there was a falling off in the rate of production of over 20 millions of tons, and a more than proportionate decrease in the quantity consumed per head of the population.† It is to be fervently hoped that such disastrous disputes between the mining population and their employers may for the future be averted

---

* 'Mineral Statistics' for 1895, p. 28.

† Thus in 1892 the proportion per head amounted to 3·737; in the following year (that of the strike) it fell to 3·300, but on the resumption of mining in the Midlands in the following year it rose to 3·754, while the total output of coal rose from 164,325,795 to 188,277,525 tons. During the strike the poorer classes of the districts affected suffered great privations from the want of fuel.

by some process of arrangement short of the arbitrament of a strike, in which both parties come off losers. Such often only terminate after the miner and his family have been reduced to penury, the owners have suffered severe financial losses, trade has been dislocated generally, and many thousands of workers, who have had no direct connection with the disputants, have been obliged to undergo severe privations through the stoppage of the factories and workshops. Nor do the results end here; for it often happens that trade is diverted from the district in which the stoppage of mining takes place, never to return. Meanwhile, coal-pits which have been kept open by their owners without profit, or even at a loss, in the hope of better times, are now closed and never again reopened. It is greatly to be desired that the system of the sliding scale adopted in South Wales and Durham were extended over the whole of the mining districts of Great Britain. By this system the miner's wage is regulated by the average price of coal; rising and falling with the price according to a graduated scale. This system has been proved in South Wales to be of the greatest benefit to both employers and employed, giving a source of certainty regarding the rate of wages, and doing away with any necessity for strikes or lock-outs in order to determine what the scale of wages is to be for a definite period.

The Low Price of Coal.—It doubtless appears to

many as a matter difficult of explanation that the price of coal continues very low, sometimes scarcely remunerative to the producers, notwithstanding the great and annually increasing demand. The cause, however, is not far to seek; and is, in fact, due to over-production. If we go back a few years in the history of coal-mining, we find a clear illustration of the statement made above, regarding the dependence of coal produce on the demand for iron. From the commencement of the year 1880, or the middle of 1879, and extending into 1883, there occurred a period of extraordinary prosperity in the iron trade; such as it never attained before or since. The output of British iron ore reached 18 millions of tons, and for the smelting of this enormous quantity there sprung up a corresponding demand for coal; while new furnaces arose all over the iron-producing districts of the midland and northern counties. Capitalists began to think that this prosperity was to be continuous for an indefinite period, and new collieries were commenced in fresh districts, generally on a large scale, as the coal had to be reached at ever increasing depths.

Meanwhile the coal-production increased by about 30 millions of tons between the middle of 1879 and that of 1883; and just as many of these new collieries had come into operation, or, as also happened, before some of them had even reached the coal-seams to be worked, a collapse in the iron trade set in, and the demand steadily declined, till the production of ore fell from its maximum of 18 millions of tons in 1882 to 13 millions in 1887; a fall of 5 millions of tons in about 5 years.* Meanwhile the new collieries once commenced, or just opening out, could not be closed without the loss of interest on the capital employed in their construction, and inevitable deterioration in the plant and machinery. There was nothing for it but to proceed in working the coal; and thus the output of this mineral continued at the level reached in 1883, while the originating cause of the increased demand had to a large extent disappeared. The consequence has been that, ever since this partial collapse of the iron trade, the quantity of coal thrown annually on the market has been in excess of the demand; prices have gone down to the extent that even the increased demand of winter has only slightly raised the value of house coal. With low prices for the commodity there must necessarily be low wages for the producers. It is gratifying, however, to observe from the returns of the Board of Trade that a revival has set in, both in the demand for iron and for coal, and the outlook seems, for the present at least, highly encouraging.†

* 'First General Report on the Mineral Industry, U.K.,' by C. Le Neve Foster, Office of Home Department, 1895.
† 'Memorandum of the Labour Department of the Board of Trade' for Nov. 1896. See APPENDICES II. and IV.

The Average Depth of Coal-Mining.—There is a question of interest with reference to our coal resources which ought not to be omitted in a treatise of this kind; namely, the average (or mean) depth at which coal is worked in our mines at the present time. In the early days of this industry the coal-seams were worked either by adits driven into the ground at the outcrop of the seams, or by shallow shafts worked by pulleys coiled round a wooden wheel called "a whimsey," and driven by horses. When the steam engine was introduced, and the portions of the seam near the surface were worked out, deeper shafts were sunk, and, instead of the horizontal "whimsey," the ropes were passed over a drum worked by machinery. The hempen rope gradually gave place to the chain for winding the buckets, and the chain to the wire rope, which for very deep shafts is flat and tapering, and is the most serviceable hitherto invented. Meanwhile, the pits were being sunk deeper and deeper as the shallower portions of the seams of coal became exhausted, till at the present day coal is drawn from depths of 3000 feet in some of our collieries in the north of England by means of very powerful machinery, which, in order to raise the necessary quantity to the surface within the period of working hours, has to be driven at high speed.

Such being, in a few words, the history of the progress of coal-mining from early times to the present day, it will be clear that in every coal-field, or district producing the mineral, there will be a certain zone of depth at which the greatest quantity of coal is raised; and this zone will constantly advance in the direction of the dip of the strata, as mining progresses. Every coal-field contains shafts of varying depth; some are deeper than others, and turn out greater or less quantities of coal. But there must be, as the general result, a certain zone of depth at which the maximum quantity is extracted for the time being. Having a few years since taken some pains to investigate this subject, I have come to the conclusion that at the close of this century our main supplies of coal will be drawn from depths varying from 300 to 400 yards; at least in our larger and more important coal-fields, such as those of Lancashire, Derbyshire, Staffordshire, Denbighshire and South Wales. In the next century these depths will be greatly exceeded; shallower collieries will be fewer in number; and for the demands of commerce and general purposes we shall have to rely on the output of mines of great depth, worked by powerful machinery and elaborate plant, and calling forth all the ingenuity and skill of managers fully instructed both in the theory and practice of mining.

Plan upon which the Resources of the Coal-fields have been determined.—Before proceeding to give the estimates of the individual coal-fields of Great Britain it will be necessary to state the course of procedure generally adopted and the bases upon which the estimates are founded. In nearly all cases the estimates arrived at by the Royal Coal Commission in 1870 have been adopted, after making deductions for quantities credited to seams of coal under two feet in thickness, which I consider ought to have been omitted from the calculations of the Commissioners. This will materially alter the quantities in some districts; but I venture to think will render the estimates of our coal-resources more reliable. The same modification will necessarily apply to the estimates of quantities outside the visible coal-fields which are concealed beneath the Permian and Triassic formations; and as considerable light has been thrown upon the question of the presence or absence of coal in such positions, by means of borings and sinkings made during the past quarter of a century, advantage will be taken of this knowledge from time to time. The next step has been the reduction of the quantities determined by the Commissioners by the amount of coal extracted from each coal-field since 1870. This amount has been obtained by adding together the yearly output as given in the returns sent to Her Majesty's Secretary of State for the Home Department by the Mine Inspectors of each district, and supplied to them by the owners or managers of the mines. These returns, published in 'The Mineral Statistics of the United Kingdom,' come down to the year 1895; but in order to include the four remaining years of the century I have added the estimated amount based on the most recent returns of output from each district; this estimate, given in round numbers, though not strictly correct, will be a sufficiently close approximation where large quantities are dealt with.* The sum thus obtained being deducted from the quantity remaining in 1870 or, where the estimate has already been made, will give approximately the available quantity at the close of the century.

The coal-fields of Ireland are included in the estimates of resources; but the produce of these districts is unfortunately too insignificant to have any effect, and is only of local interest in such an enquiry; the quantity of coal raised from all the mines of that country in 1895 only amounting to 125,586 tons.†

---

* The statistical Returns are made under the Coal Mines Regulation Act, 1887, by which a Return has to be sent annually from every mine, and from every quarry more than 20 feet deep, to the inspector for the district, specifying the quantity of mineral obtained. The statistics are prepared from these statutory returns.

† 'Mineral Statistics,' p. 27. I have, however, repeatedly pointed out that in Co. Tyrone there is a tract extending to the borders of Lough Neagh overspread by Triassic and Tertiary strata, under which a valuable coal-field may be supposed to lie, and capable of yielding a good supply of bituminous coal. The reader is referred to my 'Physical Geology of Ireland,' 2nd edition, 1891, p. 61, and to the Geol. Survey Memoir 'On the Tyrone Coal-field,' by E. T. Hardman, 1877.

CHAPTER II.

CLASSIFICATION OF BRITISH COAL-FIELDS.

THE British Coal-fields may be conveniently arranged under the following divisions, based to some extent on topographical grounds, as well as on others which are of a physical and geological character.*

I. ENGLISH COAL-FIELDS.

Midland Group.—1. North Staffordshire; 2. South Staffordshire; 3. Leicestershire; 4. Warwickshire.

North Midland Group.—1. Yorkshire, Derbyshire and Nottinghamshire.

Great Northern Group.—1. Durham and Northumberland; 2. Cumberland.

North Western Group.—1. Lancashire and East Cheshire; 2. Coalbrook Dale (or Shropshire); 3. Forest of Wyre.

---

* The Returns of the output of the coal-fields are arranged in the 'Mineral Statistics' according to county divisions; this has rendered a re-arrangement according to the areas of the coal-fields necessary, involving additional calculations.

Western Group.—Bristol and Somersetshire; 2. Forest of Dean.

II. WELSH COAL-FIELDS.

1. South Wales Basin; 2. Denbighshire; 3. Flintshire.

III. SCOTTISH COAL-FIELDS.

1. The Clyde Basin; 2. Midlothian; 3. Haddington; 4. Fifeshire; 5. Ayrshire; 6. Lesmahago; 7. Canobie.

CHAPTER III.

ENGLISH COAL-FIELDS.

MIDLAND GROUP.

This group of four distinct coal-fields occupies a position in the heart of England, and is included in the counties of Stafford, Leicester, Warwick and Worcester. The valleys of the Trent and Derwent at Nottingham and Derby mark the boundary between the Midland and the North Midland groups on the map, while it is quite certain that there is no physical connection between them underneath the Triassic strata occupying the plain of the Trent.* Recent borings have also tended to show that, not only is this group of coal-fields strictly limited towards the north by the occurrence of much older formations, but that

---

* On reading a paper (Trans. Fed. Inst. M.E., vol. xi. p. 9) at the meeting of the Confederated Institute of Mining Engineers at Sheffield in 1896, on the "Eastern Limits of the Midland Coal-fields," I was taken to task for excluding the coal districts of Yorkshire, Derbyshire and Notts from the Midland group; I find, however, that a similar distinction is adopted by Mr. C. Le Neve Foster in the 'First Annual General Report on Minerals' for 1894, p. 9.

towards the south the coal-measures are terminated by very old pre-Carboniferous formations, overlain by Triassic strata, occupying the district between Nuneaton and Ashby-de-la-Zouch; while from various considerations it would also appear that a ridge of old rocks, curving round from the Clent Hills towards the east, probably protrudes northwards towards Barr Beacon under the New Red Sandstone of Birmingham; thus partly separating the productive coal-measures of Warwickshire from those of South Staffordshire. All these considerations tend in the direction of restricting, to a greater extent than was supposed some years ago, the concealed extension of the coal-fields under the east of England.*

1. THE NORTH STAFFORDSHIRE COAL-FIELD.

This coal-field is one which ranks highest in the Midland group, both for the large number of valuable seams of coal and ironstone which it contains, as well as for their regular and uninterrupted range over large tracts.

Along the northern and central portions of the

* "The Eastern Limits of the Midland Coal-field," Trans. Fed. Inst. M.E., vol. ii. p. 9, 1896. The spur of concealed Silurian rocks inferred to pass northwards under the New Red Sandstone of Birmingham probably terminates under (or near) Barr Beacon, so that to the north of this point the coal-measures of Staffordshire and Warwickshire may be physically connected.

coal-field the strata have been thrown into a double fold along synclinal and anticlinal axes, which converge towards an apex at Congleton Edge; while in the opposite directions they diverge till, at their southern margin between Longton and Madeley, they are several miles apart. All along their southern margin from Audley, by Madeley, Keel, Newcastle-under-Lyne, Stoke and Longton, the coal-measures pass under Permian and Triassic strata, and consequently there are large stores of mineral fuel remaining undisturbed for future use;—though at great depths. From the existence of large china and earthenware factories near some of the towns above-named, the district is sometimes known as "The Potteries." A deep bore-hole has recently been put down at Hanford, on the estate of the Duke of Sutherland, which has succeeded in reaching "the Great Row" coal after passing through the thick series of the Upper Coal-measures.

Resources.

There are few coal-fields in the United Kingdom which, in proportion to their extent, are so richly stored with beds of ironstone and coal, and which, owing to the conditions stated above, give promise of such high productiveness in the future; but, notwithstanding these advantages, the output of coal has not materially increased during the last twenty years. In 1880 the yield of coal amounted to 4,074,800 tons, and in 1895 to 4,613,640 tons; but in the years 1891-92 the production exceeded 5,000,000 tons from about 145 collieries.*

In the following estimate of resources, I adopt that of the Commissioner, the late Sir George Elliot, who was assisted by Mr. W. Cope and Mr. W. Y. Craig, in preference to one by myself, showing smaller results, but probably less reliable.

1. Area of coal-field (exclusive of the Cheadle and Goldsitch basins) . 75 square miles.
2. Total thickness of strata with coals 5000 feet.
3. Number of workable seams over 2 feet in thickness about 25, with a total of available thickness of coal amounting to . . . 140 feet.
4. Available quantity down to 1880 after deducting one-tenth for thin seams . . . . . 3,312,000,000 tons.
5. Quantity worked between 1880 and 1895 . . . . . 77,316,000 „
6. Estimated quantity to be worked from 1895 to end of 1899 (in round numbers) . . . 20,000,000 „
7. Available at end of century for future use . . . . . . 3,214,684,000 „

One remarkable feature in regard to this coal-field is the circumstance that several beds of ironstone, varying from one to four feet in thickness, occur as roofs to the coal-seams, so that both can

* Min. Stat. U.K., p. 27. The estimates for "several small outlying districts" are here omitted as being unimportant; these are Cheadle, Wetley and Goldsitch.

be worked together; this is the case with the "red shag," the "red mine," the "brassy mine," and the "billy mine" seams.*

2. THE SOUTH STAFFORDSHIRE COAL-FIELD.

This coal-field was one of the earliest to be opened out in the Midlands to any large extent, owing to the occurrence therein of the thickest seam of coal in England, known as the "ten yard" or "thick seam," which over a considerable area is at a shallow depth, and crops out round Dudley and Bilston. The coal-field stretches from Brereton and Cannock Chase on the north to the Clent Hills on the south; and on either side is bounded by "down-throw faults," by which the Permian and New Red Sandstone formations are brought into juxtaposition with the coal-measures. It includes a portion of East Worcestershire, and from its centre rise the Silurian beds, forming the isolated hills of Dudley Castle and Sedgley Beacon, 760 feet high. Mining operations have within recent years been carried outside the coal-field proper, at Cannock on the west side, and at Hamstead and Sandwell Park on the east. At this last-named colliery, which is the nearest in situation to Birmingham, the "thick

---

* A description of this coal-field, with map and complete section of the coal-series, will be found in 'The Coal-fields of Great Britain,' 4th ed., p. 179.

coal," with a thickness of 8 yards, is worked at a depth of 418 yards;* but, as stated by Mr. H. W. Hughes, the coal shows a tendency to split up and diminish in thickness in an easterly direction towards Birmingham, owing probably to an approach towards a ridge of old rocks, which may be ultimately proved to pass under that town. The ridge of ancient concealed rocks considered as protruding to an unknown distance northwards, keeps to the eastward of these collieries,† and is referred to by Mr. Hughes in a recent communication.‡

Resources.

In the estimates of the resources of this coalfield, undertaken by Mr. John Hartley, assisted by Mr. Daniel Jones, those of Coalbrook Dale, the Clee Hills, and the Forest of Wyre in Shropshire, are included, amounting together in 1870 to 1,906,119,768 tons. In this figure are also included certain areas not easily defined, outside the limits of the coal-fields themselves. Under these circum-

---

* For a description of this coal-field the reader is referred to the memoir by the late Professor J. B. Jukes, Mem. Geol. Survey, 2nd ed.; and to 'The Coal-fields of Great Britain,' p. 165.

† See remarks by Mr. A. H. Stokes, H.M. Inspector of Mines, in Trans. Fed. Inst. M.E., vol. ii. p. 19 (1896); also on 'Search for Coal over the Eastern Boundary Fault,' by Mr. F. G. Meacham, ibid., vol. viii.

‡ 'Mineral Resources of South Staffordshire,' Journ. Iron and Steel Inst., No. 2, vol. xlviii. (1895).

stances, which would make any deduction as regards the resources of the South Staffordshire district by itself impossible, I think it better to bring down the estimates to the close of the century on the lines I have formerly adopted,* and which are as follows:—

1. Area of the coal-field . . . 93 square miles.
2. Average thickness of workable coal above 2 feet in thickness . . 50 feet.
3. Estimated quantity of coal remaining in 1870 north of the Bentley fault . . . . . 768 millions of tons.
4. Do. do. south of the Bentley fault 205 ,,
5. Total quantity in 1870 . . 973 ,,
6. Deduct quantity worked out between 1870 and 1895 (about 221 millions), leaving (1895) . 752 ,,
7. Deduct estimated quantity from 1895 to end of century . . 36 ,,
8. Leaving for future use in 1899† . 716 ,,

3. THE LEICESTERSHIRE COAL-FIELD.

This small, but valuable, coal-field occupies a position to the south of the Valley of the Trent, having in its centre the historically famous town of Ashby-de-la-Zouch. Along the west and south it is bounded by strata of Permian and Triassic age; along the north, by Lower Carboniferous beds, older

---

* 'Coal-fields of Great Britain,' p. 177.

† In dealing with large quantities in which some of the items are only approximately accurate, only round numbers are considered necessary.

than the coal; and along the east by the ancient slates, porphyries and volcanic agglomerates of Charnwood Forest. The central portion consists of Lower unproductive coal-measures which divide the productive district of Moira from that of Coleorton; and in both these districts the coal-measures pass below the formations of Permian and Triassic age. There are many points of great geological interest connected with the Leicestershire coal-field which it would be out of place to discuss here, as we are only concerned with its resources in coal.* It may be stated, however, as pretty well proved, both by physical considerations and by experiments in boring, that the Carboniferous strata of this part of England were deposited along the borders of a land area formed of Cambrian and Lower Silurian (or Ordovician) rocks, which presented an irregular outline towards the north, throwing out successive spurs with intervening bays in which the coal-measures were deposited as the whole region was subsiding. The rocks of Charnwood Forest and Bardon Hill formed a portion of this ancient Carboniferous land, though they have subsequently been relatively elevated along great lines of "fault," or dislocation; and as the Carboniferous strata, wherever they approached their original margin towards the

* For geological details the reader is referred to Mammat's 'Geological Facts,' and 'The Geology of the Leicestershire Coalfield,' Mem. Geol. Survey (1860).

south and east of the area of deposition, necessarily became thinner, we are able to account for the diminution in thickness of these strata in the Leicestershire area as compared with that of their representatives in Derbyshire and Yorkshire. The occurrence of these spurs of pre-Carboniferous rocks, and the general proximity of the land area formed of them in this part of England, has considerably diminished the extent of the coal-strata underlying the Triassic districts to the south, west and east of the visible coal-field; so that it is improbable that there is much coal remaining intact beyond that at present being worked under the New Red beds of either the Moira or Coleorton districts. This is a point of much importance in our enquiry into the coal resources of Leicestershire.

Resources.

The estimate of the resources of the Leicestershire coal-field furnished by the Royal Coal Commission were entrusted to the able hands of the late Mr. J. T. Woodhouse, and are in excess of those previously made by myself. This is partly owing to the inclusion of seams under two feet in thickness, according to the rule laid down by the Commissioners themselves; for this excess I have made the necessary deductions.*

---

* Rep. Coal Commission, vol. i. p. 30. Some of the seams are much injured, and to a certain extent destroyed, by the presence

1. Area of productive coal-field and of proved areas under the Permian and Triassic . . . .   20 square miles.
2. Number of workable coals from 2 feet and upwards ten, with a total thickness of (about) . . .   40 feet of coal.
3. Quantity of coal remaining for use down to the year 1870 (in round numbers) . . . . .   339,575,000 tons.
4. Deduct quantity worked from 1870 to 1895 (in round numbers) . .   30,500,000 „
5. Deduct estimated quantity from 1895 to 1899 . . . . .   6,000,000 „
6. Leaving available for future use at the end of the century . . .   303,075,000 „

4. The Warwickshire Coal-field.

This is the nearest of all the coal-fields to the metropolis. It stretches in a southerly direction from Polesworth to the east of Exhall for a distance of 15 miles, when it passes below the Triassic strata, and has been followed as a concealed coal-field to Wyken Colliery and for some distance southwards. The strata dip towards the west, except at the northern apex, where they form a trough with a reverse dip towards the east; and they pass below an extensive tract of Permian beds stretching from Baxterley

of sandstones replacing the coal, known as "rock-faults," both in the Moira and Coleorton districts. By some oversight the quantity of coal available in 1880, as given in 'The Coal-fields of Great Britain,' is excessive, but may have been intended to include large areas outside the visible coal-field referred to above.

to Coventry and Warwick. This tract, which has an area of 90 square miles, is underlain by coal-seams at a depth probably not greater than 2500 feet in any part. How much farther south than the present workings of Wyken Colliery the coal-seams stretch it is impossible to say; but the probabilities are that they will be found to terminate against an irregular bank of Silurian rocks somewhere under the valley of the River Avon.*

The investigation into the resources of this district was entrusted to Mr. J. T. Woodhouse, one of the Commissioners, whose estimates I adopt, after making a slight reduction for thin seams; the depth is under 3000 feet for the whole quantity.†

Resources.

1. Area of the coal-field, both visible and partly concealed beneath the Permian beds . . . . . 30 square miles.
2. Thickness of coal varies from . . 26 to 30 feet.
3. Net available tonnage (1870) . . 455,470,000.
4. ,, ,, (1880) . . 440,000,000.
5. Deduct quantity worked out from 1870 to 1895 . . . . . . 23,725,000.
6. Deduct estimated quantity from 1895 to end of century . . . . 8,500,000.
7. Leaving for future use at end of century 407,775,000.

---

* For further details regarding the structure of this coal-field the reader is referred to Mr. Howell's memoir 'On the Geology of the Warwickshire Coal-field,' Mem. Geol. Survey; and 'The Coal-fields of Great Britain,' p. 232 (1881).

† 'Report Coal Commission,' vol. i. p. 31.

The Warwickshire coal-field is only slowly progressive as regards its output, notwithstanding its advantageous situation for the London market; the quantity raised in the year 1880 being 1,101,386 tons, and in 1895, 2,165,410 tons; but as the value of coal rises, additional collieries may be expected to be established over the area of the Permian formation, resulting in a larger output.*

It was formerly generally believed that the coal-seams of Warwickshire extended below the Permian and New Red Sandstone of the Birmingham district into the South Staffordshire coal-field, with no interruption except such as is due to faults of more recent date than those formations themselves. But evidence begins to accumulate that, in a southerly direction at any rate, and in the Birmingham district, concealed ridges of pre-Carboniferous rocks protrude northwards through the coal-measures from the great central barrier of such rocks which crosses England from Salop and Worcestershire into East Anglia. No fewer than three such spurs have now been discovered by mining operations west of Birmingham; and it is, therefore, not improbable that similar irregularities may exist under the tract between that city and Coventry, owing to which the beds of coal will be found to terminate towards the south. Doubtless, there ex-

* Mr. F. A. Newdigate, M.P., is opening a new colliery near Arley, which will command a large area of coal.

isted a physical connection between these coal-fields to the north of the tract of country here indicated, but it would be very hazardous to speculate on the occurrence of coal south of a line drawn from Birmingham to Coventry. On this subject the communication by Mr. H. W. Hughes, with Professor Lapworth's observations thereon, is very suggestive.*

* *Supra cit.*, p. 33.

CHAPTER IV.

ENGLISH COAL-FIELDS—continued.

NORTH MIDLAND GROUP.

1. THE YORKSHIRE, DERBYSHIRE AND NOTTINGHAMSHIRE COAL-FIELD.

THIS great tract of coal-producing strata, though occupying portions of three counties, is physically one coal-field. It is the largest coal-field in England, having an area of 760 square miles between the Millstone Grit on the one side, and the Magnesian Limestone of the Permian formation on the other; while its extension eastward below newer formations is probably considerably greater. Its absolute limit in the direction of the sea-coast has not yet been proved, and is possibly beyond determination by boring experiment, owing to the great and increasing thickness of the overlying Secondary strata. But the recent successful boring at South Carr, near the banks of the Trent, by which the "Barnsley Hard" coal, nearly five feet thick, was penetrated at a depth of 3181 feet, proves that the coal-measures stretch considerably eastward of this position.* There seems every probability on geological grounds that the North Midland coal-field is but the visible portion of a great basin, the eastern side of which is concealed by newer formations. This question I have elsewhere discussed at some length, and it is a view generally accepted by geologists.† Along the north and west the limits of the coal-field are well determined by the uprising of the Millstone Grit; but at its southern extremity near Nottingham, the coal-field passes below the New Red Sandstone and marl, along the valley of the Trent, and sweeps round to the eastward, so that there is no physical connection between it and the coal-field of Leicestershire. All along the eastern margin the escarpment of the Magnesian Limestone forms the boundary of the visible coal-field; but coal is now worked below this formation in several collieries. The first colliery to pierce this formation being that of Shire Oak, where the full thickness of the Permian beds was found to be 207 feet.‡

* Trans. Fed. Inst. M.E., vol. xii. (1896). Another deep boring in advance of coal-mining was put down at Scarle, near Lincoln, some years ago, when Carboniferous strata were pierced at a depth of 1900 feet, but their actual position in the formation was not satisfactorily determined. See 'Coal-fields of Great Britain,' p. 260.

† 'Coal-fields of Great Britain,' 4th ed., p. 259; Prof. Ramsay, Rep. Coal Commission, vol. i. pp. 136–8; Prof. A. H. Green, *ibid.*, vol. ii. p. 504; Mr. W. S. Gresley, 'On the Yorkshire and Notts Coal-field, &c.,' Trans. Fed. Inst. M.E., vol. ii. (1896) p. 134.

‡ Messrs. Lancaster and Wright, Quart. Journ. Geol. Soc., vol. xvi. p. 137.

As regards future mining operations, there can be no doubt that there are great resources in store, not only in the visible coal-field, but extending below the Triassic and Permian formations. The progress of mining ever tends eastward, as the shallower seams are being worked out along the western parts of the coal-area; and the sequestered haunts of Robin Hood amidst the oaks of Sherwood Forest are destined ere long to be invaded by the miner's shaft. The new "East and West" Railway, opened on the 19th November, 1896, between Chesterfield and Lincoln, will also open out a large coal district in Nottinghamshire, on the estates of the Dukes of Portland and Newcastle, of which the surface is overspread by New Red Sandstone and conglomerate, and for which deep shafts and powerful machinery will be required, in order to win the underlying seams of coal.

Resources.

VISIBLE COAL-FIELD.

1. Area of coal-field west of the escarpment of the Magnesian Limestone . . . . 760 square miles.
2. Greatest thickness of productive coal-measures, including the lower series . . . . 4500 feet.
3. Average number of workable coal-seams above 2 feet in thickness, 15; giving a total thickness of coal of . . . . . 46 feet.

4. Quantity of coal down to a depth of 3000 feet available for use	13,327,784,000	tons.
Quantity from 3000 to 4500 feet	420,348,000	,,
Total	13,748,132,000	,,

CONCEALED.

5. Quantity of coal down to 3000 feet	4,374,830,000	,,
Quantity from 3000 to 4500 feet	283,835,000	,,
Total	4,658,665,000	,,
6. Total of quantity in visible and concealed areas after deducting one-tenth for thin seams, and excess of depth over 4000 feet, leaving available in 1870	16,566,118,000	,,
7. Quantity approximately worked between 1870 and 1295	769,416,000	,,
8. Estimated quantity from 1895 to end of 1899	176,000,000	,,
Total quantity worked between the years 1870 and 1889	945,416,000	,,
9. Quantity of available coal at end of century for future use, estimated at	15,620,702,000	,,

The produce of this great coal-field is increasing "by leaps and bounds," as will be seen by the following figures. In 1859, the output amounted to 12,497,100 tons; in 1869, ten years later, to 17,865,367; in 1880, to 29,810,033 tons; and in 1895, to 39,831,862 tons. This is largely due to the excellent quality of the coal, which is partly bituminous, and partly "free burning," or suitable for steam purposes.*

* Woodhouse, Rep. Coal Commission, vol. i. p. 30. Some of the harder seams have the "splint" structure.

CHAPTER V.

ENGLISH COAL-FIELDS—continued.

THE GREAT NORTHERN COAL-FIELDS.

1. DURHAM AND NORTHUMBERLAND.

THIS coal-field is sometimes known under the name of "The Great Northern," or "The Newcastle" coal-field, this town having been the principal shipping port for the coal-trade from the earliest times. It extends from the mouth of the Coquet on the north, to Staindrop near the north bank of the Tees on the south, a distance of about 50 miles. Its greatest diameter is near the centre, along the course of the Tyne; and, from the mouth of this river at South Shields the coal-measures pass below the escarpment of the Magnesian Limestone and Yellow Sandstone of the Permian formation, which becomes the eastern margin of the visible coal-field to the banks of the Tees. Coal is now largely worked by shafts sunk through the Permian formation all over its area; while it is also followed under the bed of the North Sea by a few collieries at Blyth in Northumberland and Monk Wearmouth and Whitburn in Durham.* The Millstone Grit forms the western and southern limit to the coal-measures; but beds of coal are worked throughout Northumberland in strata below the Millstone Grit, though they are not sufficiently important to be included in the general estimate of the coal-resources.†

In estimating the resources of this coal-field I have been unable to separate those of the visible from the concealed areas.

Resources.‡

1. Area of the visible coal-field . . 460 square miles.
2. Area of coal-measures concealed below the Permian and New Red Sandstone . . . . 225 ,,
3. Number of workable seams from 18 inches upwards, giving a thickness of . . . . 46 feet of coal.

---

* From information kindly furnished by Mr. J. L. Hedley, Inspector of Mines.

† For further information regarding the structure of this coal-field the reader is referred to Mr. Dunn's memoir 'On the Northern Coal-field,' Trans. N. of Eng. Inst. M.E., vol. xii.; also 'The Coal-fields of Great Britain,' 4th ed., p. 269.

‡ The resources of the Durham coal-field were estimated for the Coal Commission by Sir George Elliot, and those of Northumberland by Mr. Thomas E. Forster, Report, pp. 20–25. They both included all seams of 12 inches and upwards. All the seams are within a vertical depth less than 4000 feet. Coal was also included under the sea for a distance of $3\frac{1}{2}$ miles from the coast, but it seems very doubtful if much of it could be workable for such a distance, inasmuch as there are grounds for believing that

NORTHUMBERLAND.

4. Available coal on land after necessary deductions for loss, &c. (1870)	2,744,896,000 tons.
5. Available under the sea for a distance of 3½ miles	403,200,000 ,,

DURHAM.

6. Available coal on land, including seams 12 inches in thickness (1870)	3,988,853,000 ,,
7. Available under the sea for a distance of 3½ miles	2,234,500,000 ,,
Total in round numbers (1870)	6,223,350,000 ,,
8. Deduct for thin seams under 2 feet one-tenth, leaving available in 1870	5,601,015,000 ,,
9. Deduct quantity worked from 1870 to 1895	894,513,000 ,,
10. Deduct estimated quantity worked to end of 1899	38,000,000 ,,
11. Leaving available at end of century	4,668,502,000 ,,

The coal is of excellent quality, suitable for gas, steam and iron smelting; the output is progressive, amounting, in 1880, to 34,913,508 tons, and in 1895 to 39,827,905 tons, of which Durham produces about two-thirds. With an output of 40 millions of tons per annum the coal-field would be exhausted in a

the seams of coal rise and crop out under the waters, in consequence of which they would be unworkable where they reach shallow depths below the sea-bed. The deduction of one-tenth is intended to correct this inferred excess, as likewise that owing to thin seams.

little over a century. This serious consideration will occupy us further on; I content myself with calling attention to it here.

2. Cumberland.

This coal-field occupies the northern and western slopes of the mountains of the Lake District, and is bounded by the waters of the Solway Firth and the Irish Sea, under which the coal-measures stretch for unknown distances, while the coal extracted from the land and below the sea is largely shipped from the ports of Whitehaven, Silloth and Maryport. From Maryport to Bolton by Crosby and Aspatria the coal-measures are overlain by Red Sandstones of Permian age, under much of which the coal is workable, and is probably connected with the little coal-field of Canobie, in Scotland, below the estuaries of the Esk and Eden. There are in all about seven workable seams of a greater thickness than 2 feet, giving an average thickness of 35 feet of coal.

Resources.

1. Area of the productive coal-measures . . . . . 25 square miles.
2. Available quantity on land and for 2 miles out to sea in 1870[*] . 371 millions of tons.

---

[*] Estimate of Mr. Forster, Rep. Coal Commission, vol. i. p. 21, after deducting estimate for quantity under 24 inches, amounting to 33,982,433 tons.

3. Deduct quantity worked from 1870 to 1880 (about) . . . 15 millions of tons.
4. Deduct quantity worked from 1880 to 1895 . . . . . 28,078,000 tons.
5. Deduct estimated quantity to end of 1899 . . . . . 7,400,000 ,,
6. Leaving for future use at end of century . . . . . 320,522,000 ,,

The output from the Cumberland coal-field is slightly progressive, the quantity raised in 1880 from 31 collieries being 1,680,840 tons, and in 1895, 1,883,590 tons; in 1859 it only amounted to 1,041,890 tons. Cumberland has become a great centre for the manufacture of the highest class of iron, since the discovery of the large deposits of hæmatite in the underground caverns of the Carboniferous Limestone.

CHAPTER VI.

ENGLISH COAL-FIELDS—continued.

NORTH-WESTERN GROUP.

1. LANCASHIRE AND EAST CHESHIRE.

THIS important coal-field stretches from the neighbourhood of Liverpool at Knowsley eastwards in a semicircular form by Wigan, Bolton, Oldham and Ashton-under-Lyne to Poynton near Stockport in Cheshire, with Manchester near the centre. The coal-seams have a general dip southwards in Lancashire, and westwards in Cheshire; and pass below the Permian and Triassic strata of the plain of Cheshire where these latter attain an enormous thickness.* The coal-field is bounded along the north and east by the uprising of the Millstone Grit, forming a range of hills merging in the Pennine Chain of Yorkshire and Derbyshire; and lying to

---

* A boring put down in search of coal at Marston by the Salt Union Company in 1891, did not succeed in passing through the New Red Sandstone at a depth of 2610 feet; Mr. C. E. De Rance, Trans. Fed. Inst. M.E., vol. x. p. 244.

the north of the Bolton hills is the important coal basin of Burnley, which owes its presence among the Millstone Grit uplands to the existence of a large "down-throw" fault. The whole coal-field is traversed by numerous faults, some of great displacement, and generally ranging in N.N.W. to S.S.E. directions. The coal is generally of excellent quality, suitable for household and gas-making purposes, while the "Mountain Mines" are capable of yielding strong coke.* The coal is not only used largely for house and manufacturing purposes in the immediate neighbourhood, but is largely exported from Liverpool and other ports; no less than 1,197,216 tons having been shipped from Liverpool to ports in the United Kingdom, while 416,733 tons were exported to foreign countries and British settlements in the year 1894.† In addition to the above, large quantities are sent away by rail southward. Some of the deepest collieries in the United Kingdom are to be found in the neighbourhood of Wigan, Manchester and Stockport, in which coal is worked at a depth of about 3000 feet.

* For further account of the coal-field the reader is referred to the Memoirs of the Wigan, Bolton, Manchester and Stockport districts, published by the Geological Survey; to papers by Mr. Binney, Trans. Geol. Soc., Manchester, vols. i. and ii.; Mr. Dickinson's 'Vertical Section of the Coal-Series' (1858), and 'The Coal-fields of Great Britain,' 4th edition, p. 195.

† Return by order of the House of Commons, dated 23rd August, 1895.

Resources.

1. Area of the coal-field, including the Manchester and Burnley districts . 217 square miles.
2. Total thickness of strata with coal . 6000 feet.
3. Number of workable coals above 2 feet:—St. Helens, 13; Wigan, 17; Manchester, 18; giving an average thickness of . . . . . 62 feet of coal.
4. Quantity of available coal down to 4000 feet in depth, after deducting 1-100th for seams under 2 feet in thickness (1870)* . . . . 5,490,540,000 tons.
5. Deduct quantity worked from 1870 to 1880, amounting to 181,000,000 tons, leaving (1880) . . . 5,309,540,000 ,,
6. Deduct quantity worked from 1880 to 1895, amounting to 342,219,000 tons, leaving (1895) . . . 4,967,321,000 ,,
7. Deduct estimated quantity to be worked to end of 1899 (95,200,000 tons), leaving at the end of the century an available quantity of . . . 4,872,121,000 ,,

In the above estimate the quantity remaining at the end of this century is to a large extent concealed beneath the Permian and Triassic formations, but is included within a depth of 4000 feet from the surface. The quantity estimated by Mr. Dickinson as lying between 4000 and 6000 feet is about 90 millions of tons, some of which may be recoverable. The

* Mr. J. Dickinson, one of the Commissioners, whose estimates I adopt, states that one per cent. may be deducted for seams under 2 feet in thickness; letter, dated 9th December, 1896.

output of the Lancashire coal-fields is still increasing, notwithstanding its large amount, and reached 19,802,300 tons in 1880, and 22,764,180 tons in 1895; if we assume the output at the beginning of the next century to reach 25 millions of tons, the quantity remaining to a depth of 4000 feet will last for a little over 150 years.

2. COALBROOK DALE.

The Coalbrook Dale coal-field in Shropshire is one which geologically is of peculiar interest. It has a general triangular form, with its base in the valley of the Severn, and its northern apex at Newport.[*] Along its western side it is bounded by a large "down-throw" fault which brings in the New Red Sandstone, and partly by the Cambro-Silurian rocks of the Wrekin. The general dip of the strata is eastwards, and in that direction the coal-seams pass below the Permian beds, under which they are worked by the Lilleshall Company in the northern part of the district; but from the observations of Mr. Marcus W. T. Scott [†] and Mr. Daniel Jones [‡]

---

[*] For a description of the geological features the reader is referred to the Memoir of Professor Sir J. Prestwich, Geol. Trans., 2 ser. vol. v. (1840).

[†] Journ. Geol. Soc., vol. xvii. (1861).

[‡] Geol. Mag., vol. viii. p. 200 (1871); 'Coal-fields of Great Britain,' 4th edition, p. 140. I have to acknowledge with thanks information afforded by Mr. Noel T. Beech, manager of the

there seems every probability that the coal-seams rise and terminate eastward under the Permian formation; while it has been fully established by the same observers that the upper measures have been deposited over a denuded surface of the middle and lower series. Over a large part of the southern and central portions of the coal-field the beds of coal and valuable ironstone have now been worked out; and owing to the easterly rise of the strata above referred to it seems very doubtful if any coal will be found under the New Red Sandstone of Shiffnal.

Resources.

1. Area of the coal-field . . . . 28 square miles.
2. Number of coal-seams upwards of two feet in thickness, 6; giving a total thickness of . . . . 27 feet of coal.
3. Quantity available in 1880 in the visible coal-field . . . . 12,000,000 tons.
4. Quantity available under the Permian formation (estimated) . . . 15,000,000 ,,
5. Total quantity available (1880) . . 27,000,000 ,,
6. Deduct quantity worked from the year 1880 to 1895 . . . . 11,618,279 ,,
7. Deduct estimated quantity from 1895 to end of 1899 . . . . 2,800,000 ,,
8. Leaving for future use at end of century . . . . . 12,581,000 ,,

Lilleshall collieries, conveyed through Mr. W. N. Atkinson, H.M. Inspector of Mines, regarding the workings under the Permian.

The output of this coal-field has been stationary since 1889; but, regarded for a longer period, it has been retrogressive. In the year 1880 it reached 905,000 tons, and, in 1895, 698,128 tons. There can be no doubt that the coal-field has seen its best days as regards the whole area.

3. THE FOREST OF WYRE.

This coal-field is as large in area as that of Coalbrook Dale, with which it is connected by a narrow strip of coal-measures lying along the valley of the Severn. As has been shown by Mr. Daniel Jones,* the upper coal-series with sulphurous coals are unconformable to the lower series with "sweet" seams of considerable extent and thickness.† As regards the resources of this tract, they are not very considerable, and have been included by Mr. Hartley in those of Salop and South Staffordshire, from which it is impossible to eliminate them. Probably we shall not greatly err in placing the unworked quantity of coal at ten millions of tons.

* *Supra cit.*, p. 53, also communication to the S. Staffordshire Inst. M.E. (1894), in which he correlated the Harcott and Kinlet Main coals with the "deep" and "shallow" seams of Cannock.

† More recently (1894) an interesting paper has been published by Mr. T. C. Cantrill on the Forest of Wyre district, bearing on several points of geological classification, Quart. Journ. Geol. Soc., vol. li. p. 528. Also, by the same author, 'Contribution to the Geology of the Wyre Forest Coal-field' (Kidderminster), 1895.

CHAPTER VII.

ENGLISH COAL-FIELDS—continued.

WESTERN GROUP.

1. BRISTOL AND SOMERSETSHIRE COAL-BASIN.

THIS coal-basin occupies portions of two counties, that of Gloucestershire on the north and of Somersetshire on the south; Bristol, standing in the centre of its western border, being the chief city in the district, and giving its name to the whole. It is remarkable for the extent by which it is concealed by the overspread of the Secondary formations; which, being themselves nearly horizontal in position, rest on the upturned edges of the Carboniferous strata. But, notwithstanding this partial concealment, it has been proved that the coal-formation is disposed in the form of a complete basin; as the Lower Carboniferous beds, whether visible or concealed, surround the coal-measures both on the north, south, east and west, as I have shown elsewhere.* The extreme length of the coal-basin

---

* Plate ii., 'Coal-fields of Great Britain,' 4th edition, p. 112,

from north to south is 26 miles; and its breadth, including the detached basin of Nailsea, somewhat less; along the south, the uprising of the Carboniferous limestone along the chain of the Mendips marks conspicuously the southern margin of the coal-formation.

Notwithstanding its great extent, the productiveness of this basin is greatly restricted, owing to the seams of coal being so thin that they will be unworkable at great depths; besides which, they are much bent, contorted and faulted. Owing to the fact that about half the seams have a thickness of only two feet and under, it is necessary, in estimating the future resources of this district, that large deductions from the total quantity should be made. The "Pennant" rock, which overspreads so large a portion of the lower, or Bedminster and Holcombe, series, and which has a mean thickness of about 2000 feet, will undoubtedly prove a serious obstacle to the working of the deeper seams, owing to the expense of sinking through it. None of these seams are of a greater thickness than four feet, while most of them are of a thickness varying from two to three feet. The late Professor Prestwich—who, with the

---

where a fuller account of its geological structure will be found in chap. ii.; as also in Prestwich's report, 'Coal Commission,' vol. i. p. 33; and Etheridge's 'Lecture on the Physical Structure of the Northern Part of the Bristol Coal-field.' Mr. Sanders has produced a map of the coal-field on a scale of 4 inches to the mile.

assistance of Mr. Anstie, made an elaborate series of estimates for each parish, giving a grand total of nearly 7000 millions of tons—has rightly appreciated the force of the special impediments to future mining operations, and has made considerable deductions, amounting to one-fifth of the whole, on the quantity in the lower series.* Still, I regard this as insufficient, and venture to think that a deduction amounting to one-half would be a more reliable quantity. I therefore adopt here the estimates originally arrived at by myself, at the same time putting the reader in possession of those given by this distinguished Commissioner, drawn up in accordance with the rules laid down; according to which seams of above one foot in thickness were to be included.

Resources as estimated by the Author.

1. Area of coal-basin, of which only 45 square miles are not concealed by newer formations . . . 150 square miles.
2. Greatest thickness of measures with coal . . . . . . 5125 feet.
3. Number of coal-seams, from 2 feet and upwards in thickness, 20; giving a total thickness of coal of . 71 ,,

---

* Rep. Coal Commission, vol. i. Prestwich states that none of the seams can be traced over the whole coal-field, and that every seam varies in thickness within short distances. *Ibid.*, p. 34.

4. Quantity of coal down to a depth of 4000 feet, available after making necessary deductions (1880) . . 2000 million tons.
5. Quantity worked from 1880 to 1895 amounting to 13,405,000 tons, leaving (1895) . . . . 1,986,595,000 tons.
6. Deduct estimated quantity to end of 1899—4,000,000 tons; leaving for future use at end of the century . 1,982,595,000 „

Resources as estimated by the late Professor Sir Joseph Prestwich.

Professor Prestwich's estimate of the available quantity down to a depth of 4000 feet in 1870, was 4210 millions of tons, which after making the same deductions for quantities extracted to the end of the century, would leave a supply for future use of 4184 millions of tons; being somewhat more than twice the amount arrived at by myself.

The output of this coal-basin has been almost stationary since 1880, when it amounted to 757,802 tons; in 1895, fifteen years later, the output was only 841,491 tons. Such slow increase in the output as compared with that of South Wales, and considering its advantageous position, is sufficient evidence of the difficulties of mining in this area, and appears to be some justification for the smaller estimate I have given of the future resources.

2. Forest of Dean, Gloucestershire.

This little coal-basin lies to the west of the Severn Valley, under one of the Royal Forests, and in its outline is a more perfect "basin" than any other coal-field in England, though of somewhat irregular outline. The coal-measures which lie in the centre of the basin are surrounded by hills of Millstone Grit and Carboniferous Limestone, in which occur bands of hæmatite, giving rise to an iron industry of limited extent, but producing metal of excellent quality. Some of the seams of coal, and especially the "Coleford High Delf," have suffered deterioration owing to the presence of masses of sandstone, called "horse-backs" or "rock faults," by which the coal has been cut out and replaced. As regards the resources of this basin, which in any case are small, it is impossible to form any very approximate estimate, owing to the above-named irregularities; nor can we tell exactly the amount of the annual output, as the returns sent in by the Inspector of Mines include all Gloucestershire, part of which must be credited to the Bristol district north of the Avon. The output, however, may be taken at a little under a million tons per annum.

Resources.

1. Area of coal-basin . . . . 34 square miles.
2. Number of coal-seams of 2 feet and upwards in thickness, 8; giving a total thickness of coal of . . 24 feet.
3. Quantity of coal remaining for use in 1880 . . . . . . 260 million tons.
4. Estimated quantity remaining at end of century (about) . . . . 244 million tons.

The output in 1891 of the Forest of Dean was 884,831 tons, and in 1895, 925,657 tons,* so that it may be considered progressive.

* As I am informed by Mr. Jordan of the Home Office.

CHAPTER VIII.

THE WELSH COAL-FIELDS.

1. THE SOUTH WALES BASIN (INCLUDING MONMOUTHSHIRE.)

THE coal-basin of South Wales is, with the exception of that of the Clyde Valley, the largest in Great Britain, but falls considerably short of that of the North Midland coal-field if we include the concealed area of the latter. The whole of the South Wales coal-measures are unconcealed by newer formations; but under the waters of both Caermarthen and Swansea Bays extensive areas lie submerged, where it is hopeless to expect to recover the minerals except to a very limited extent. By the latter inlet from the Bristol Channel, the coal-basin is separated into two unequal portions. That to the east of the Bay stretches to Pontypool, in Monmouthshire, a distance of 56 miles, and is the larger portion. The western portion extends to St. Bride's Bay, a distance of 17 miles, and is washed by the waves of the Atlantic. The greatest transverse diameter of the basin is 16 miles, in the meridian of Neath, in Glamorganshire, and its general form is that of an oval basin or trough, becoming attenuated westwards in its extension into Pembrokeshire. The beds rise and crop out both to the north and south, and round the eastern margin in Monmouthshire, resting on Millstone Grit, which in turn is underlain by the Carboniferous Limestone which often takes the form of high terraced escarpments, particularly along the northern outcrop.

The coal-measures east of Caermarthen Bay are traversed throughout nearly the whole of their length by a remarkable anticlinal axis, which has been traced from the north of Risca, by Pontypridd and Ton-yr-efail, across the Lesser Ogwr by Nant-Tyrus, the Maesteg ironworks and Aberavon, beneath Swansea Bay. The basin has thus been divided into a northern and southern trough, lying on either side of the great anticlinal axis, and of which the former occupies twice the area of the latter. The effect of this axis, or saddle, is to bring the lower coals within ultimate reach of mining operations along a considerable tract of country. It should also be noted that this line of elevation being placed so as to be nearer the southern side of the basin, where the inward dip of the strata is steepest, the lowest seams, which are of great value, have been placed within reach of mining operations, which otherwise would not have been the case. The general result is highly favourable for their ultimate recovery, and adds considerably to the effective resources of the whole basin of South Wales.

Another cause tending in the same direction is the existence of great valleys intersecting the whole region from north to south, and cutting deep down through the uppermost strata, which are the least productive, into the middle and lower series. It was along the sides of these valleys that mining was first commenced by means of adits driven into the sides at the out-crop of the coal-seams. Amongst these may be specially mentioned the Amman, the Tawe, the Neath, the Rhondda, the Taff, and the Ebbw. These valleys have been utilised for lines of railway, by which the produce of the collieries is carried down to the works or shipping ports of Swansea, Neath, Barry, Cardiff and Newport. Amongst these Cardiff takes the lead, owing to the excellence of the steam coal brought down from the collieries of the district traversed by the Taff Vale Railway, and the elaborate arrangements and facilities afforded for the shipment of the coal provided by the Cardiff docks; while the Great Western Railway affords facilities for rapid transport into England.

This is not the place for a description of the geological structure and special details of this great coal-basin, but a few points may be mentioned as bearing on its productiveness and future resources.*

---

* For such details the reader is referred to the Memoirs of Sir H. T. de la Beche, Mem. Geol. Survey, vol. i.; Report by Messrs. Vivian and Clark, Roy. Coal Commission, vol. i.; 'Coalfields of Great Britain,' 4th edition, chap. i. pt. 2 (1881). A fresh survey is now in progress by the officers of the Geological Survey U.K., on a scale of 6 inches to the mile.

The total thickness of the coal-formation reaches to no less than 11,600 feet, and it will therefore be clear that some of the seams of coal, where the higher strata form the surface near the centre of the basin, are far beyond the reach of mining industry. Still, many of these seams are rendered accessible owing to the depth of the valleys by which the strata are traversed. Another impediment to mining is the occurrence of the thick beds of sandstone, already referred to in the account of the Bristol coal-basin, and known as the "Pennant Grit," which attains a thickness of about 2000 feet. The third, and last peculiarity I shall refer to is the remarkable change which the character of the coal-seams undergoes when followed from their eastern margin in Monmouthshire to their western extremity in Pembrokeshire. In the former position the seams of coal are bituminous, in the latter they occur as anthracitic, while in the central region of Glamorganshire they are chiefly semi-bituminous, giving rise to the qualities most favourable for steam-generating purposes, and hence known as "steam coal." This is the fuel used in the Royal Navy, and exported to coaling stations in many seaports throughout the globe.

Resources.

The estimate of the resources of the South Wales Basin which I originally made of available coal down to a depth of 4000 feet, amounted to 24,000 millions of tons, of which I considered 16,000 millions available in the year 1870. For these I now substitute those of Messrs. H. H. Vivian and G. T. Clark, who have produced, with the help of several assistants, tables showing the quantities at various depths.* In adopting these estimates, however, I have found it necessary to make several modifications, as follows:—

1. I have omitted the quantity credited to the "Crowsfoot vein," which does not exceed a thickness of 2 feet, and is generally under it.

2. I have omitted the amount of coal placed under the head of "doubtful and under the sea."

3. I have made a deduction of about one-third in "Group XI.," which includes the seam called "stinking," or sulphurous, as being unfit for use except for very local purposes. These deductions reduce Messrs. Vivian and Clark's estimates from (in round numbers) 19,280,000,000 to 16,973,000,000 tons.† The estimates thus modified will give the following results:—

MESSRS. VIVIAN AND CLARK'S ESTIMATES MODIFIED.

Quantity down to 2000 feet	10,273,000,000 tons.
,, from 2000 to 3000 feet	3,953,000,000 ,,
,, ,, 3000 ,, 4000 ,,	2,747,000,000 ,,
Total (1870)	16,973,000,000 ,,

* Rep. Coal Commission, vol. i.
† In dealing with such large quantities, round numbers only are adopted.

Quantity worked from the years 1870 to 1880 (about) . . .	200,000,000 tons.
Quantity worked from 1880 to 1895	434,417,000 ,,
Estimated quantity to be worked to end of 1899	166,000,000 ,,
Leaving available for future use at end of the century . . .	16,172,583,000 ,,

From the above figures it will be seen that since the year 1870 down to the close of the century about eight hundred millions of tons will have been extracted.

The output of coal has rapidly increased of late years; the quantity raised in 1880 amounted to 21,203,743 tons; in 1890, ten years later, to 29,372,853 tons, and in 1895, to 32,513,325 tons. This is chiefly from collieries situated in the counties of Glamorgan and Monmouth; the quantity of coal raised in the counties of Caermarthen, Pembroke and Brecon being comparatively insignificant. The quantity shipped from Newport, Cardiff, Barry, Swansea and other ports, chiefly for steam purposes, amounted to 14,755,475 tons in 1894, and the remainder of the output is consumed in iron-works, tinplate works, railway fuel and household purposes. A considerable quantity is also sent into England by rail, and shipped to British and Irish ports.

Some of the collieries are of great depth; of these the following may be specially mentioned [*]:—

---

[*] For particulars of which I am indebted to Mr. J. T. Robson, Inspector of Mines for South Wales.

The Albion at Pontypridd, 545 yards; the Avon at Abergwynfi, 511 yards; the Bedlinog, Dowlais, 565 yards; the Deep Navigation, Treharris, 718 yards; the Lady Windsor, Pontypridd, 593 yards; the Ferndale, No. 8 shaft, 460 yards; the Penrikyder at Mountain Ash, 530 yards, and the Resolver at Neath, 540 yards; some of these mines are working coal under the additional depth of over 300 feet, due to the height of the mountains above the level of the shaft.

2. Denbighshire Coal-field.

This coal-field commences about three miles south of Oswestry, where the New Red Sandstone rests directly on the Millstone Grit, having overlapped transgressively both the Permian and coal-measures in that direction. From this southern termination the coal-field extends northwards by Oswestry, Ruabon and Wrexham to the valley of the Alyn, which winds through a deep defile, and exposes in its banks an almost complete section of the upper beds of the coal-formation. The northern extremity of the coal-field is defined by the line of "the great Bala fault," a remarkable line of fracture which, ranging in a E.N.E. direction from the Lake of Bala, crosses the valley of the Alyn near Hope, and produces a complete break between the Carboniferous strata of Denbighshire and Flintshire. The length of the coal-field is about 18 miles, and it is about 4 miles in breadth at Wrexham. The coal-measures rest on the Millstone Grit, which rises in a high escarpment facing the west above the Vale of Llangollen, and they pass below the Permian and New Red Sandstone formations of the plain of Cheshire towards the east. They contain several valuable seams of coal worked in deep collieries, one of which at Hafod near Ruabon, has a depth of 500 yards; the coal finds its way to market through the Great Western Railway and its branches.*

Resources.

1. Area of the visible coal-field . . 47 square miles.
2. Number of workable seams of 2 feet and upwards, 7; giving a total thickness of . . . . . . 30 feet of coal.
3. Quantity of coal remaining unworked to a depth of 4000 feet (1870) † . 1,287,000,000 tons.
4. Deduct quantity worked from 1870 to 1895, about . . . . . 20,000,000 „
5. Deduct estimated quantity to be worked down to the end of 1899, say 10 millions of tons; leaving for future use at end of the century . 1,257,000,000 „

The production of coal from the Denbighshire coal-field has been slowly progressive, but is capable

* For fuller details of the Denbighshire coal-field the reader is referred to the maps and sections of the Geological Survey; the 'Coal-fields of Great Britain,' 4th edition, p. 149.

† Estimate of Mr. Dickinson, Rep. Coal Commission, vol. i.

of a much larger increase. The output in 1869 amounted to 1,427,701, tons; in 1880, to 1,650,410 tons; and in 1895, to 2,207,000 tons. The value of the seams of coal is enhanced by the regularity with which they are distributed for long distances, with a steady dip towards the east.

3. THE FLINTSHIRE COAL-FIELD.

This coal-field stretches from the "great Bala fault" above described to the banks of the estuary of the Dee, where it attains its greatest breadth of 15 miles. Like the Denbighshire coal-field, it rests on a foundation of Millstone Grit, and passes below the New Red Sandstone of the Cheshire plain directly, without the intervention of the Permian beds. The coal-measures of this district rarely attain any great depth, owing to the existence of numerous faults, ranging generally from north to south, along which the beds are repeatedly upheaved, with the result that the seams of coal have been brought so near the surface as to be largely denuded away, or actually worked out. As a matter of fact, this coal-field is rapidly undergoing exhaustion, especially in the case of the "Main" and "Hollin" seams, which are the most valuable; and the whole district is so "faulty" that it does not pay to work the coal when prices are low. For the same reason also the lower seams, which are thin, have remained unproved over considerable areas; while the "cannel" seam, once so valuable, owing to its richness in oil, has been worked out, and a line of abandoned oil-works near Mold attest the destruction of a former profitable industry. There can be little doubt that the coal-measures pass below the estuary of the Dee and the New Red Sandstone north of Chester; but owing to the great thickness of this formation and the extent to which the coal-measures were disturbed, faulted, and denuded before the New Red Sandstone was deposited upon them, there can be no certainty regarding the presence of workable coal-seams in any special locality until they have been determined by boring experiments, and those of great depth. The time has certainly not yet arrived for attempting such experiments.

Resources.

1. Area of the coal-field and portion of concealed area . . . . 35 square miles.
2. Number of workable seams about 6, giving a thickness of . . . 35 feet of coal.
3. Unwrought and available quantity of coal, including the tract along the estuary of the Dee, and the coalfield of Neston in Cheshire, in 1870[*] . . . . . . 700,000,000 tons.

---

[*] The estimate of Mr. Dickinson in 1870 was 718 millions of tons, including Neston in Cheshire; from the statements above it will be inferred that this estimate is somewhat excessive, and I have made a small deduction in consequence; even with this reduced figure the quantity is probably too large.

4. Quantity of coal raised between 1870 and 1885, 25,167,110 tons, leaving available (in round numbers, 1885). 674,000,000 tons.

5. Deduct estimated quantity to end of 1899, about 3,200,000 tons, leaving available at the end of the century . 678,000,000 ,,

The output of this coal-field is stationary or retrogressive. In 1880 it amounted to 779,000 tons, in 1890 to somewhat less, and in 1895 to 641,079 tons.

Detached Coal-areas.

In passing from the consideration of the resources of the Welsh and Salopian coal-fields, it should be stated that there are several small detached areas to which no special reference need be made as far as regards their mineral resources, though geologically they are of great interest. These are the coal-fields of Anglesea, the Clee Hills north of Ludlow, of Shrewsbury, and Le Botwood. It would be beyond the scope or intention of this treatise to do more than refer to them here, as our enquiries are directed to those districts only in which the quantity of coal can be considered of importance in connection with the general resources of the country.

CHAPTER IX.

THE SCOTTISH COAL-FIELDS.

POSITION AND DIVISIONS.

THE Carboniferous strata of Scotland occupy the great valley lying along the estuaries of the Clyde and Forth, bounded towards the north by the slopes of the Grampian Mountains, and along the south by those of the Southern Uplands. The coal-bearing portions consist, not only of the strata which represent the coal-fields of England and Wales, but also those which belong to the Yoredale beds and Carboniferous Limestone series; thus Scotland enjoys an advantage in this respect which is not shared by the sister country to the south of the border.*

The coal-fields of Scotland are separated from each other by the uprising of older strata belonging to the "Calciferous series," and by enormous masses of volcanic rock, such as that which forms the Renfrewshire Hills, separating the coal-field of the Clyde Basin from that of Ayrshire. They are thus divisible

---

* Except to a small extent in Northumberland, where the geological conditions approximate to those of central Scotland.

into the following coal-fields, which alone are of importance as regards our inquiry * :—1. That of the Clyde Basin; 2. Mid-Lothian and Haddington; 3. Clackmannan; 4. Fifeshire; 5. Ayrshire; 6. Lesmahago; and 7. Dumfries-shire.

1. The Clyde Basin.

The coal-field of the Clyde Basin includes portions of Renfrewshire, Dumbartonshire, Stirlingshire, and nearly the whole of Lanarkshire, and is traversed throughout its entire length by the river Clyde, along the banks of which, above Glasgow, fine sections of the strata are laid open, especially at Hamilton and the Falls of the Clyde. Glasgow is its central city, and owes its prosperity to the abundance of coal and ironstone of the Clyde Valley. From this city, all along the river side to Greenock, is presented a remarkable spectacle of the industrial energy of the people developed in the direction of ship-building, such as is not to be seen anywhere else throughout the world.

The coal-series of the Clyde Basin contains from ten to twelve seams of workable coal, above two feet in thickness, and several bands of "clay-band" and "black-band" ironstone, besides a bed of cannel, or "gas coal," which was at one time worked under

* I exclude the little coal tracts of Argyll, Sutherland and Roxburgh, which, though of geological interest, are economically unimportant.

the northern side of Glasgow itself. The "Hurlet" is the lowest seam of workable coal, 5 feet in thickness, but of inferior quality. The whole series is about 4000 feet in thickness.* It was in this district that the "black-band" ironstone was first utilised by David Mushet, early in the present century.

2. THE MID-LOTHIAN AND HADDINGTON COAL-BASINS.

These coal-areas occur in the form of a double trough, the deeper of which lies in Edinburghshire on the west, and the shallower in Haddington on the east. The axis of the deeper trough passes nearly north and south under the town of Dalkeith, and on approaching the Carberry ridge the beds rise and crop out; while the Roman Camp Limestone forms a dividing ridge been the two troughs. East of the city of Edinburgh the shores of the Firth of Forth are the northern margin of the coal-basins; but the seams of coal and their accompanying strata pass to an unknown distance under the bed of the Firth.†

* For further information on this and other districts, the reader may consult the Geological Survey Memoir on the Lanarkshire Coal-field; Mr. W. Moore's communication to the Philosophical Society of Glasgow; Mr. John Geddes' 'Report, Royal Coal Commission,' vol. i. p. 71; and 'The Coal-fields of Great Britain,' 4th edition, p. 286.

† For further information on this coal-district the reader is

3. THE FIFESHIRE COAL-FIELD.

This coal-field, throughout its eastern half, lies along the northern shore of the Firth of Forth, and may be physically connected with the Lothian basin; but its productiveness, which for its size is considerable in regard to the number of the seams of coal, is greatly reduced, owing to the intrusion of igneous rocks. The necks of many old Carboniferous, or Permian, volcanoes, which poured forth lava over the sea-bed, or vomited showers of ashes, lapilli and bombs, can even now be identified, and their effect has been greatly to injure the seams of coal with which they come in contact, and generally to reduce the productiveness of the whole Carboniferous area. There are about twenty-five seams of coal of a thickness of two feet and upwards, and of qualities suited for the production of gas, steam, and for iron smelting; there is a total combined thickness of about 110 feet of coal.*

4. THE CLACKMANNAN COAL-FIELD.

This coal-field is disunited from that of Fifeshire by the uprising of the Lower Carboniferous rocks

referred to the Geol. Survey Memoir, by Messrs. Howell and Geikie.

* For an account of this coal-field, see Mr. Landale's 'Trans. of the Highland Society,' vol. xii.

near Dunfermline. It stretches along the northern and eastern banks of the river Forth, by which it is separated from the great central coal-field of the Clyde Basin. It contains ten seams of coal of a thickness of two feet and upwards. According to Mr. Geddes, the southern portion of the coal-field was largely worked out in 1870; the middle area was extensively worked, and the northern portion was comparatively entire north of the river Devon; these three divisions are separated by considerable faults. The maximum thickness of the combined seams amounts to about 120 feet of coal.*

5. The Ayrshire Coal-field.

This coal-field stretches along the coast of the Irish Sea from Ardrossan to the mouth of the river Doon, and extends inland to the base of a range of trappean hills, by which it is separated from the Carboniferous tract of the Clyde Basin. It is a rich and productive district, large quantities of coal being shipped from the ports of Ayr, Troon, Irvine and Ardrossan. Owing, however, to the presence of large masses of old volcanic rock of Carboniferous age, and the intrusion of dykes and sheets of basalt, a large portion of the minerals have been burnt and destroyed, and mining is sometimes attended with uncertainty or loss. There are four or five work-

* Rep. Coal Commission, vol. i. p. 76.

able seams of coal, giving a total thickness of about 20 feet; much of the coal has already been worked out.

6. Lesmahago Coal-basin.

The detached basin of Lesmahago and Douglas lies to the south of the great Lanarkshire coal-field, and consists of strata very low down in the Carboniferous series; the coal-seams are generally thin and of inferior quality, and the district is chiefly known for its celebrated bed of "gas coal," which has now been largely worked out.

7. Dumfries-shire Coal-basins.

This border county is enriched by the presence of two small coal-fields or basins, those of Sanquahar and Canobie; the former lying along the valley of the Nith, the latter in the depression formed by Eskdale and Liddesdale, on the borders of the Cheviots. These detached coal-basins are bordered by Silurian rocks forming the southern uplands of Scotland; and in the case of the Canobie coal-field, the coal-measures are overlain by Permian beds and have a general dip southward towards the northern shore of the Solway Firth, under which there is probably a physical connection with the coal-measures of Cumberland. The Canobie district contains seven seams of coal of a greater thickness than three feet, giving a total of 36 feet of coal; but of these, the two uppermost are already exhausted. The Sanquahar Basin is less productive.

Resources of the Scottish Coal-fields.

The estimates of the resources of the coal-fields of Scotland were entrusted to Mr. John Geddes, one of the Commissioners, whose great knowledge acquired in the profession of mining engineer was ably brought to bear upon this important subject; and his conclusions would be accepted with confidence if we also accepted the data on which they are based. But there are three points upon which, as it appears to me, we must make considerable deductions from the large figure, amounting to 9,843,456,930 tons, of the total available quantity of coal remaining to be worked and recoverable in 1870.* They are as follows:—

1. In the first place, it would appear that Mr. Geddes' estimates include seams under two feet in thickness; sometimes as low as 12 or 14 inches, as shown by the sections of different districts upon which the estimated quantities are based;† this was in accordance with the rule laid down by the Commissioners, to which I have already stated my objections. It is impossible to say exactly what deduction should be made for such seams, as in some

---

* Rep. Coal Commission, p. 77.
† For example, that of Loanhead, p. 72.

districts they bear a large proportion to the total thickness of the coal-seams; as, for example, in the cases of Tannochside, Wishaw and Colburn, while in others the proportion is small; but we shall probably be safe in assuming the amount to be not less than one-twentieth of the whole.

2. The second point is one of opinion, and is therefore one on which Mr. Geddes' views are entitled to great weight, namely, the extent to which coal can be recovered under the Firth of Forth. The inference he has arrived at, that there are very large stores of coal under this estuary between the Edinburgh coal-field on the south and that of Fifeshire on the north, can scarcely be disputed; but the further inference that this coal is recoverable to the extent of 1800 millions of tons, extending for 10 miles out to sea,* is one which must be regarded with great hesitation. The view is not supported by experience. The extent of mining under the sea in the north of England has made very little progress of late years.† Much depends on the direction and amount of dip of the strata in determining whether the water can be kept out of the mines at considerable depths and under corresponding pressure.

---

* Report, p. 75.

† Out of all the collieries in Cumberland, Northumberland and Durham, only two in Cumberland, and one in each of the other counties work coal under the sea, as I am informed by Mr. John L. Hedley, H.M. Inspector of Mines; 16th December, 1896.

Where seams rise and crop out under the sea—as would be the case under the Firth of Forth—the water would tend to find access along the planes of the strata; and should cracks or fissures arise from subsidence over the hollows from which the coal has been extracted, flooding of the mines would be inevitable. In any case extensive barriers would be necessary, to keep out the water between the outcrop and the workings, and where the roofs of the coal-seams, or the strata lying in proximity to the roofs, consist of porous sandstone, it is probable that they are saturated with water. For these reasons, chiefly, I regard the future working of coal-seams to any large extent under the sea as impracticable; and only otherwise when at great depths and under favourable conditions. These are points on which there will be considerable differences of opinion; but as it bears on our present enquiry, I feel bound to make a very large deduction from the estimates given under this head by the Commissioners, amounting to about one-half of the whole quantity.

3. The third point requiring reduction is of minor importance, but it is necessary to mention it. Three coal-fields have been included with a total quantity accredited to them of 10,793,620 tons; they are those of the counties of Argyll, Sutherland and Roxburgh. They are all insignificant in extent and productiveness, and need scarcely be included in an

enquiry bearing on the mineral resources of the whole of Scotland.

With the above deductions the estimate of resources in 1870 is reduced to (in round numbers) 8486 millions of tons.

In stating these resources as they may be at the end of the century, it will be necessary to give the general result for the whole of the Scottish coal-fields, because the returns in the "Mineral Statistics" are stated according to counties, and it would be somewhat difficult to apportion them to their respective coal-fields.

The production of coal has been on the whole highly progressive, as will be seen by the following statement :—

Production in 1859 amounted to 10,300,000 tons.
,, 1878 ,, 17,837,282 ,,
,, 1880 ,, 18,274,886 ,,
,, 1890 ,, 24,278,589 ,,
,, 1895 ,, 28,792,700 ,,

The above rapid increase is due to the extent and variety of uses to which the coal is applied, including the domestic supply of the great towns, the smelting and manufacture of iron, chemical works, steam purposes, ship-building, manufactures and exportation.*
In 1895, 1,048,774 tons of pig-iron were smelted from 2,331,664 tons of ore, at an expenditure of

* In the year 1894 there were exported from Glasgow and Greenock 612,012 tons of coal.

1,971,731 tons of coal, being less than two tons of coal to one of pig-iron. Glasgow has for long been one of the great centres of the iron trade, and until the rise of Middlesborough it had no competitor, and the prices there quoted ruled the market. The occurrence of iron-stone under the forms of "clay-band" and "black-band" in conjunction with coal gave the original impulse which developed into the great trade of the nineteenth century.

Resources.

1. Quantity of coal remaining in 1870, and available for future use, modified from Mr. Geddes' estimates   8,486,000,000 tons.
2. Quantity worked between the years 1870 and 1880 (approximate) .   200,000,000 ,,
3. Quantity worked between 1880 and 1895 . . . . .   363,360,717 ,,
4. Estimated quantity to be worked up to end of the year 1899 . .   115,000,000 ,,
5. Quantity of available coal left for use at end of the century . .   7,807,640,000 ,,

It should be mentioned that, with the exception of parts of the Lanarkshire Basin about Hamilton, Waddington and Blantyre, all the coal-seams of Scotland are at a less depth from the surface than 4000 feet, and, therefore, within the generally accepted workable limit. It is doubtful, however, if any but the best seams, both as regards quality and thickness, will be mined beyond 3000 feet. Mr. Geddes does not suppose that in any case the depth will exceed this last-named figure, and he truly remarks that " large capital will be required to undertake such depths of winnings, and the price of coal must range higher than at present." When he wrote the greatest depth did not exceed 1200 feet.

* Report, p. 78.

CHAPTER X.

COAL SOUTH OF THE THAMES.

THE presence of coal under the tract south of the valley of the Thames has, for many years past, been inferred by geologists, and has recently been demonstrated as a fact by the experimental boring carried out under the superintendence of Mr. Francis Brady, engineer of the Channel Tunnel, in a position at the foot of Shakespeare's Cliff, near Dover, in 1895-6.* In this borehole a seam of "good bituminous coal" was reached at a depth of 2177 feet from the surface and of a thickness of 4 feet; a discovery of unquestionable importance from a local point of view. Whatever may be the future history of coal-mining in the south of England, the boring experiment at Dover will be ever memorable as the first in which

---

* 'The Kent Coal-field,' by F. Brady, M. Inst. C.E.; G. P. Simpson and N. R. Griffith, Trans. Fed. Inst. M.E., vol. xi p. 540. See also papers by Prof. Boyd Dawkins, Lecture at the Royal Institution, 6th June, 1890; Trans. Manchester Geol. Soc., vol. xxi. (1892), and *ibid.*, vol. xxii. (1894); Marcel Bertrand, 'Correlation of the Coal-fields of Northern France and Southern England,' Trans. Fed. Inst. M.E., 1893.

the views of the late Mr. Godwin-Austen, Sir Joseph Prestwich and of other geologists, regarding the presence of coal under this tract were put to the test of experiment ;—and were confirmed.*

From several papers descriptive of the strata passed through by the Dover boring we gather that the Cretaceous strata extended down to a depth from the surface of 1157 feet, and that below this the coal formation was penetrated through a thickness of 1173 feet without reaching the base. Several seams of less thickness than three feet were passed through until the 4-feet seam was reached. From the analysis of this coal it would appear to belong to the class of semi-bituminous or "steam coals," as it contains 83·8 per cent. of carbon, and it is thus comparable with the coals of this class derived from South Wales. There is, therefore, every prospect that the working of this seam will prove of great advantage, not only to the town of Dover and to the railways in connection with it, but also to the steamers plying across the Channel.

As regards the question of the probable area underlain by the coal-formation to the south of the valley of the Thames, there can be little doubt that it is considerable, and that the coal-measures have assumed the form of a trough, the axis of which

---

* Godwin-Austen, Quart. Journ. Geol. Soc., vol. xii. (1855); Prestwich, Rep. Royal Coal Commission, vol. i. p. 146, in which the subject is fully discussed.

trends westwards in the direction of the southern border of the Somersetshire coal-field to the north of the Mendips; and eastwards, under the Straits of Dover towards Calais. This view has been generally adopted by geologists; but in the evidence which I gave on this question before the Royal Coal Commission in 1870 I pointed out that it was probable that this trough has been broken into several detached portions by tranverse N.—S. flexures, or axes, of later date than the disturbances which had produced the trough itself;* and recently the observations of Professors Rücker and Thorpe seem to give confirmation to this view, as indicating the existence of old magnetic rocks under the Windsor area. Sir J. Prestwich, however, was unable to accept these views to the extent to which I advanced them, but should mining operations proceed westwards from Dover time will show whether or not they are correct.† But it may now be accepted as geologically certain that between Dover and Bath there occurs a more or less interrupted trough of coal-measures of 150 miles in length, and of a breadth

* Report, vol. i. pp. 147 and 156; Proc. Roy. Soc., Dec. 22 (1870).

† In the map to 'The Coal-fields of Great Britain,' 4th edition, I have indicated by a dotted line the supposed position of the coal-trough. This was published in 1881, about ten years before the boring experiment. But it will be observed on reference to the map itself that I had correctly placed the line as passing through Dover.

varying from two to four miles measured from north to south.

Judging by the cores brought up from the Dover boring, the strata passed through are nearly horizontal, from which it would seem that the centre of the trough has been pierced. But, judging by the condition of the representative strata in Belgium on the one hand, and along the northern flanks of the Mendip Hills on the other, the coal-measures must be generally highly inclined, flexured and sometimes possibly inverted. That this southern tract of coal-strata can, to any large extent, compensate for the gradual exhaustion of our Midland and Northern coal-fields, is not to be anticipated. We cannot seriously look forward to the day when our great manufacturing centres of Lancashire, Yorkshire, Derbyshire and Notts will be transferred to the lovely slopes and wooded vales of Kent, Surrey and Hants! It will probably be a good many years before the output of the Kent collieries reaches two millions of tons per annum, and then it will only amount to one-hundredth part of the British coal-production. Meanwhile, we shall watch with interest the progress of this experiment in the opening up of the coal-resources of this new district, which is in a fair way of being carried out, as a pair of shafts are now being put down by which to work the mine; and amongst the solved problems and remarkable discoveries of the nineteenth century will rank, as not of least importance, that of the real existence of "A Kent Coal-field." *

* While I write the syndicate formed for opening out this coal district are carrying on their operations with energy. We learn from the *Bullionist*, 16th January, 1897, that the 17-feet shaft is completed and lined with brick down to a depth of 560 feet, and the 20-feet shaft to 250 feet, while large quantities of powerful plant have already been delivered at the works. By the end of January the new pumping machinery will be erected and in full working order, and the sinking of the shafts is at the rate of 6 feet per day. The syndicate has already acquired sufficient mineral rights to justify the formation of at least three pairs of shafts of similar calibre to those now being put down; and in order to determine the direction in which the coal-trough extends inland, it is proposed to put down five additional trial borings.

A sad accident has impeded the fulfilment of the above expectations (April, 1897).

CHAPTER XI.

SUMMARY OF ESTIMATED RESOURCES OF THE BRITISH COAL-FIELDS AT THE CLOSE OF THE NINETEENTH CENTURY, THE COAL-FIELDS BEING ARRANGED IN ORDER OF THEIR CONTENTS OF COAL DOWN TO A DEPTH OF 4000 FEET FROM THE SURFACE.

Order of Coal Contents.	Name of Coal-field or Group.	Quantity in tons at end of century down to 4000 feet.
1	South Wales basin	16,172,583,000
2	North Midland group	15,620,702,000
3	Scottish group	7,807,640,000
4	Lancashire and Cheshire group	4,872,121,000
5	Great Northern (Northumberland and Durham)	4,668,502,000
6	North Staffordshire coal-field	3,214,684,000
7	Bristol and Somersetshire basin	1,982,595,000
8	Denbighshire coal-field	1,257,000,000
9	South Staffordshire coal-field	716,000,000
10	Flintshire coal-field	678,000,000
11	Warwickshire coal-field	407,775,000
12	Cumberland coal-field	320,522,000
13	Leicestershire coal-field	303,075,000
14	Forest of Dean basin	242,000,000
15	Coalbrook Dale coal-field	12,501,000
	Total quantity	58,275,700,000

I have not considered it necessary to add the quantities from the Irish coal-fields, which I estimated in 1870 to contain an available quantity of 182,280,000 tons. The output from all the coal-fields of this island in 1895 only amounted to 125,586 tons—quite insufficient to supply the local demand. The production is stationary, and falls much short of the amount which the coal-fields are capable of producing if worked with a little more enterprise, especially in Co. Tyrone, where there exists a concealed area of considerable extent and resources between Coal-island and the shores of Lough Neagh.* In 1870 I estimated the quantity of coal in this partially concealed coal-field at 27,000,000 tons.†

* See the Author's 'Physical Geology and Geography of Ireland,' 2nd ed., p. 60 (1891).
† Rep. Coal Commission, i. p. 144.

CHAPTER XII.

BRITISH COAL-RESOURCES.

1. QUANTITY OF AVAILABLE COAL UNDER THE PERMIAN AND TRIASSIC FORMATIONS.

THE coal-formation of these Islands is known to exist under two conditions: one, in which it occupies the surface and forms a "visible coal-field, or basin"; the other, in which it is overlain by newer divisions under which the formation passes, and thus forms a "concealed coal-field." We have already considered the resources of the former, and it now remains to consider those of the latter, where the strata are known to lie within workable depth. The greater number of the English and Welsh coal-areas occur under both conditions, where the visible coal-fields pass below the Permian and Triassic (or New Red Sandstone) formations, and have for many years been worked to some extent by shafts passing through the newer formations into the coal-measures. Amongst these may be mentioned especially the Somersetshire, Lancashire, Midland and North Midland districts. As time goes on, and our collieries pass from the shallower into the deeper districts of mining, the quantity of coal raised from beneath the newer "Secondary" formations will tend to increase; at present it does not amount to probably more than one-tenth of the whole quantity raised.

The question how far the coal-measures extend under the Triassic and Permian formations in England, is one of great importance and much difficulty, especially in the central counties. The Royal Coal Commission of 1870 very properly turned its attention to the subject, and took the opinions of several geologists specially qualified to advise upon it; and the task of drawing up the report of the Commission was entrusted to the able hands of the late Sir Andrew C. Ramsay, at that time Director of the Geological Survey of Great Britain.* Within the last quarter of a century, however, much new light has been thrown on the subject, owing to the sinking of new collieries and of trial borings over the areas occupied by these more recent formations, with the general result that the extension of the coal-formation below the New Red Sandstone and Permian has been found to be less extensive than was supposed when the Commission was pursuing its investigations; and hence, on account of this, as well as on other grounds presently to be stated, considerable reductions will have to be made in the figures set down to represent the resources of these concealed areas.

* Report, vol. i. p. 119.

In revising these results, and endeavouring to bring them into accord with our present knowledge, I have been obliged to eliminate quantities of coal, the existence of which was in some cases admitted by Sir A. C. Ramsay himself to be doubtful, or speculative, and also to make deductions on the ground that seams of coal under two feet in thickness are included, in accordance with the rule laid down for the guidance of the various reporters by the Commissioners themselves.*

In estimating the quantity of coal in several of the coal-fields as given above, it will be observed that the amount of coal under the adjoining areas of Permian and New Red Sandstone has already been included down to depths of 4000 feet from the surface, the limit of depth here adopted. These are 1, Leicestershire (in part) ; 2, Warwickshire ; 3, North Midland,† Great Northern coal-field,‡ Lancashire and Cheshire, Coalbrook Dale, Bristol and Somersetshire.

We may commence this part of our enquiry by stating with confidence that all experiments by boring and sinking shafts in the eastern counties go to confirm the views held by myself and other geologists for many years past, that coal-measures do not exist under the part of England extending from the

* Rep., p. 142.
† Including Yorkshire, Derbyshire and Nottinghamshire.
‡ Including Durham and Northumberland.

Wash and the coast of Norfolk on the north to the valley of the Thames on the south. The borings, which have been put down at Stutton in Suffolk, Orton in Northampton, Bletchley in Bucks, Lutterworth in Leicestershire, Harwich in Essex,[*] and Ware in Herts,[†] have passed through newer formations into those much more ancient than the coal-formation.[‡] If there had been coal-measures under this tract, it would have been proved ere this by one or more of these boring experiments. What they do appear to show is as follows:—

Under Norfolk, Suffolk, Bucks and adjoining districts, the Cretaceous strata are underlain by rocks of Cambrian or Lower Silurian age. Proceeding southward into Hertfordshire, Upper Silurian rocks, with fossils identified by Mr. R. Etheridge, have been pierced under the same Secondary strata; further south still, under London and the Thames Valley,

[*] It was once supposed that in this boring "Carboniferous slate," with *Posidonia*, had been penetrated, but this view has since been abandoned, or at least questioned.

[†] J. Hopkinson 'On the Discovery of Silurian Rocks in Hertfordshire,' Trans. Watford Nat. Hist. Soc., vol. ii. part 7 (1880).

[‡] Mr. W. Whitaker, in his Presidential Address to Section C, at the meeting of the British Association at Ipswich in 1895, makes the most of what can be said in favour of coal being found in the eastern counties. But at that very time a boring had been put down at Stutton, entering rocks of hard purple unfossiliferous grit and slate, which the writer has examined, and believes to be of Cambrian or Lower Silurian age—much more ancient than the coal-formation; similar rocks were penetrated to at Lutterworth, &c.

Devonian strata, also identified by fossils, have been reached, thus giving a general succession from older to newer formations as we proceed southwards. According to this arrangement, it may be inferred that under the line of the North Downs and Weald Clay, the Carboniferous Limestone, which in Belgium is of great thickness, lies hidden, giving place in its turn to the band of coal-measures which has been successfully reached by boring at Dover, as described in a previous page.* These successive formations of Palæozoic age may be supposed to range themselves in somewhat parallel bands, from east to west; from the eastern, into the midland, counties. Having thus determined the eastern and southern limits of the non-productive region, we have now to ascertain the northern and western limits. This subject I have recently treated in detail in a paper published in the Transactions of the Institute of Mining Engineers, which, as it is easily accessible, will render it unnecessary for me to do more than give the general conclusions here.†

The Midland coal-fields of North and South Staffordshire, Warwickshire and Leicestershire appear to have a very limited extension under the Triassic and Permian beds towards the east and south. In these directions the coal-measures are terminated against

---

* P. 85.

† On 'The Eastern Limits of the Midland Coal-fields,' Trans. Fed. Inst. M.E., vol. xi. p. 9 (1896).

a shelving face of land formed of Cambrian and Lower Silurian rocks, which, appearing in Shropshire and North Wales, passes under the newer formations along the southern margin of the Dudley coal-field; and then, curving round towards the north, reappears in Leicestershire. This general line appears to have been very irregular in form, consisting of a succession of ridges projecting towards the north-west, separated by intervening bays or depressions in which the coal-measures were deposited, and thus are found stretching southwards beyond the general margin.* The coal-seams of Wyken, near Coventry, and of Bagworth, in Leicesterhire, seem to have been deposited in troughs of this kind. The accompanying sketch-map will show the supposed limits of the coal-measures under the concealed areas of this part of England.† With regard

---

* Some of the conclusions in Sir A. C. Ramsay's Report are vitiated by the supposition—at that time prevalent—that the Warwickshire coal-measures rest on Millstone Grit and Lower Carboniferous rocks. It has since been shown by Professor Lapworth that the latter are of Cambrian age.

† There is only one locality where, from the account of a boring given by Sir A. C. Ramsay (Rep. vol. i. p. 134), it might be supposed that coal-measures were discovered in the district left blank in the above map, and thus represented as barren ground; viz. at Sapcote, two miles east of Hinkley. But it is very clear that the 830 feet of "coal-measures" stated as passed through below 492 feet of newer strata, were really not coal-measures at all, but probably Cambrian or Lower Silurian beds. It is specially mentioned that "no beds of coal were reached,"

to the other tracts of concealed coal-measures, I propose to take them in the order in which they

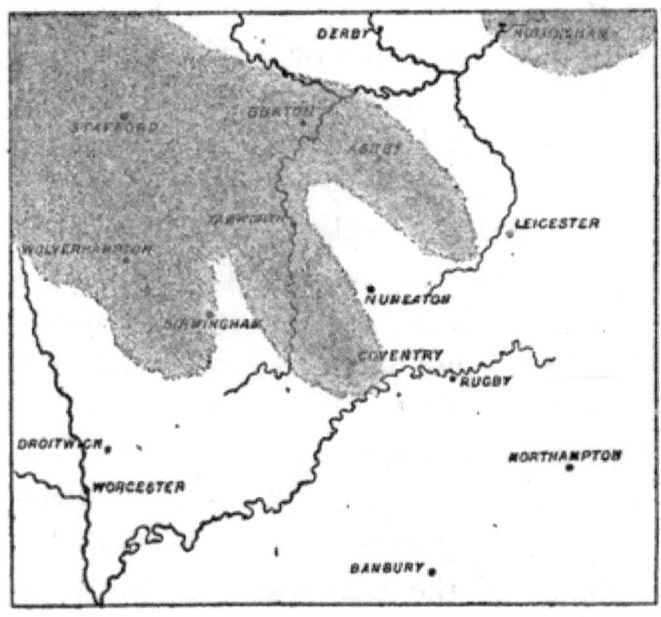

FIG. 1.—OUTLINE MAP OF THE MIDLAND DISTRICT, showing approximate Limits of the Coal-formation. Shaded portion shows coal-area both visible and concealed.

have been dealt with in the Report of the Coal Commission, giving both the estimates of resources

which would be a very extraordinary circumstance if the strata were really coal-measures. And when we recollect that the quartzites, grit and shales along the eastern margin of the Warwickshire coal-field, now known to be of Cambrian age, were at that time (1870) supposed to be of Lower Carboniferous age, it is not surprising that somewhat similar strata brought up from a bore-hole should also be mistaken for those of the Carboniferous period. The real age of the Atherstone rocks was determined by Prof. Lapworth; 'On the Discovery of Cambrian Rocks in the Neighbourhood of Birmingham,' 'Geol. Mag.,' vol. ix. p. 563.

as therein stated, and those which on full consideration I have substituted, together with the reasons for the modified estimates. The districts reported on by Sir A. C. Ramsay are arranged as follows *:—

2. SUMMARY OF AVAILABLE AMOUNT OF COAL UNDER PERMIAN AND OTHER OVERLYING FORMATIONS AT DEPTHS OF LESS THAN 4000 FEET, 40 PER CENT. BEING DEDUCTED FOR LOSS AND OTHER CONTINGENCIES (Rep. p. xi.).†

Districts.	Formation.	Square Miles.	Tons of Coal.
1. Warwickshire	Permian	73	2,165,000,000
2. ,, south of Kingsbury	Triassic	5	150,000,000
3. ,, north of Atherstone	,,	6	179,000,000
4. Leicestershire, Moira district	Permian	15	1,000,000,000
5. ,, Coleorton district	Triassic	25–28	790,000,000
6. Tract between Warwickshire and South Staffordshire coal-fields	Pm. & Tr.	116	3,400,000,000
7. Tract between South Staffordshire and Salop coal-fields	..	196	5,800,000,000
8. Tract between South Staffordshire and Salop coal-fields to the Cheadle and North Staffordshire coal-field	Pm. & Tr.	200	4,580,000,000
9. Tract east of Denbighshire coal-field	,,	50	2,489,000,000
10. Tract west and south-west of North Staffordshire coal-field	,,	50	1,500,000,000

* Report, vol. i. pp. xi. and 118–144. The sections are given in another volume of the Report.

† All these estimates include thin seams, which are inadmissible at great depths, and for which allowance of about 10 per cent. has to be made.

Districts.	Formation.	Square Miles.	Tons of Coal.
11. Tract in Cheshire, west of Kerridge	Pm. & Tr.	9	62,000,000
12. Tract, Cheshire, between Woodford fault and Denton	,,	36	1,790,000,000
13. Lancashire, east and west of Manchester	,,	30	350,000,000
14. Lancashire, west of Eccles and Stretford to Prescott, Runcorn and Hale	,,	130	3,883,000,000
15. Wirrall promontory, Mersey and northwards	Triassic	316	3,000,000,000
16. Yorkshire, Derbyshire and Notts	Pm. & Tr.	900	23,082,000,000
17. Vale of Eden, Ingleton, Burton, &c.	Permian	43	1,626,000,000

3. Revised Estimates of Resources of Concealed Coal-fields.

QUANTITY OF COAL.

1. *Warwickshire.**—About 15 square miles have already been included with the coal-field; and for this proportionate deduction in the resources of the Commission will have to be made, reducing the amount to . . . . . 1732 millions of tons.
2. *Warwickshire*, south of Kingsbury . 150 ,, ,,

---

* Mr. A. H. Stokes, Inspector of Mines for this district, informs me (24th December, 1890), that old Wyken Colliery is worked out and abandoned, but a new colliery has been opened and is at work. Craven Colliery, between Sow and Coventry, is the most southerly mine in the district, and in both these mines the coal is of the normal character, and exhibits no signs of approaching any original margin of old rocks, as is the case south of Dudley.

3. *Warwickshire*, north of Atherstone; from the investigations of recent years, it is almost certain that no coal-measures underlie this area; and the quantity of coal credited to it must now be excluded from this estimate * . . . .   QUANTITY OF COAL.

(coal absent).

4. *Leicestershire*, Moira district; the amount credited under this head must now be either excluded or very much reduced, owing to the results of recent borings at Nether Seal, and the condition of the main coal, which is largely replaced by bands of sandstone (say) . .   25 millions of tons.

5. *Leicestershire*, Coleorton district; a large proportion is either already worked, or is included in the resources of the coal-field above † (say) . . . . . .   500 ,, ,,

6. Tract between Warwickshire and South Staffordshire coal-fields; one-tenth is here deducted for thin coal-seams, leaving (say) .   3000 ,, ,,

7. Tract between South Staffordshire and Salopian coal-fields. This is such a wide tract of Triassic ground, and it is in such close proximity to the original margin of the coal-formation, that it is very doubtful whether it may not be partly underlain by Silurian or Old Red Sandstone, as is admitted by Sir A. C. Ramsay.‡ In the centre of

---

* See p. 96.   † P. 37.
‡ Report, vol. i. p. 122.

		Quantity of Coal.
	the basin the Trias and Permian is probably 3000 feet in thickness, while, owing to denudation, the productive coal-seams may be largely absent. A large reduction in the estimate is required, say, one-third, leaving about	3800 millions of tons.
8.	Tract between above coal-fields and North Staffordshire and Cheadle; reduction for thin seams being made, leaves about	4120 ,, ,,
9.	Tract east of Denbighshire coal-field; reduction for thin seams being made leaves about	2241 ,, ,,
10.	Tract west and south-west along border of North Staffordshire; with deduction for thin seams leaves	1350 ,, ,,
11.	Tract under Cheshire plain west of Kerridge. As it is doubtful if any coal could be reached at a less depth than 4000 feet, I omit the amount stated above	,, ,, ,,
12.	Tract between Woodford and Denton; this quantity is already partly included in the estimates for the Lancashire and Cheshire coal-field; one-half remaining (say)	895 ,, ,,
13.	*Lancashire*, east and west of Manchester; this may be considered as included in the estimates for the Lancashire coal-field	,, ,, ,,
14.	Tract west of Eccles and Stretford to Runcorn; about one-half of this has been already included in the estimate for the Lancashire coal-field, leaving about	1940 ,, ,,

15. Wirral promontory and Mersey . 3000 millions of tons.
16. North Midland coal-field; the estimate for this area is given above, along with that of the coal-field itself,* as is also that of the Great Northern, forasmuch as in both these districts coal is now largely worked under the newer formations ,, ,, ,,
17. Vale of Eden, Ingleton and Burton; a large reduction will be necessary in this case, as the thickness of the Permian Sandstone is supposed to reach 5000 feet, and it is faulted down on the north side against the coal-measures. What the depth to the coal may be west of Carlisle it is impossible to say, but in all probability over 4000 feet. In the present uncertainty of the problem we should probably not be justified in crediting the district to a greater extent than (say) . 500 ,, ,, †

4. Summary.

The following is a summary of the above revised estimates of the quantity of coal under concealed areas, in addition to that included in the estimates of the coal-fields:—

* P. 44, No. 6.
† The geological survey of the Cumberland coal-field has been completed only recently. The large amount credited to lie under the Permian beds in the Report of the Coal Commission is admitted by Sir A. Ramsay to be "mere conjecture," p. 143. I prefer to minimise the amount; and am doubtful if it would not be safer to omit even the above quantity.

		Millions of tons.
1.	Warwickshire	1732
2.	Warwickshire	150
4.	Leicestershire	25
5.	Leicestershire	500
6.	Warwickshire and South Staffordshire	3000
7.	South Staffordshire and Salop	3800
8.	Staffordshire	4120
9.	Denbighshire	2241
10.	North Staffordshire	1350
12.	Cheshire	895
14.	Lancashire	1940
15.	Wirral (Cheshire)	3000
17.	Vale of Eden	500
	Total	23,253

We have now arrived at an approximate estimate of the quantity of coal remaining to be worked at the end of the century, down to a depth of 4000 feet from the surface, based upon the results arrived at by the Commissioners; but modified by the exclusion of thin seams, and also revised, so as to bring the results into harmony with discoveries made during the last quarter of a century.

The combined results in the case of both visible and concealed areas may now be summarised.

The amount under both heads arrived at by the Commissioners in 1870 was 146,480,285,398 tons. The difference in the two estimates is due mainly to three causes. 1. A reduction from the total quantity for thin seams of coal; 2. A reduction for quantities extracted and estimated to be extracted between 1870 and 1899; and 3. A reduction for quantities under concealed areas as rendered necessary by recent investigations and discoveries.

5. TOTAL ESTIMATED QUANTITY OF COAL IN THE VISIBLE AND CONCEALED COAL-FIELDS, WITHIN A DEPTH OF 4000 FEET, REMAINING AT THE CLOSE OF THE NINETEENTH CENTURY.

	Tons.
1. Quantity remaining in the visible coal-fields of Great Britain and partially-concealed areas	58,275,700,000
2. Quantity in the entirely concealed areas	23,253,000,000
Total quantity under both areas	81,528,700,000
Add estimated quantities in the Irish coal-fields (visible and concealed)	155,300,000
Total for the United Kingdom	81,683,000,000

CHAPTER XIII.

The following table gives the quantity of coal raised in the different coal-fields for the year 1895, as returned to the Home Office by Her Majesty's Inspectors of Mines.*

Order.	Name of Coal-field, or Group.	Output in Tons. 1895.
1	South Wales basin	33,040,114
2	North Midland Group (Yorkshire, Derbyshire and Nottinghamshire	40,671,673
3	Lancashire and Cheshire group	22,764,171
4	Great Northern coal-field	39,827,804
5	North Staffordshire	4,613,640
6	South Staffordshire	7,920,552
7	Warwickshire	2,165,410
8	Leicestershire	1,467,292
9	Forest of Dean	925,657
10	Coalbrook Dale and Forest of Wyre	698,128
11	Bristol and Somersetshire	1,478,914
12	Denbighshire	2,206,993
13	Flintshire	641,079
14	Cumberland and Westmoreland	1,884,605
15	Scottish group	28,792,693
16	Irish group	125,586
	Totals for the United Kingdom	189,574,311

* The returns issued by the Home Office are arranged in counties. The re-arrangement into coal-fields is here attempted, but there is a slight difference in the results—amounting to 87,051 tons—for which I am unable to account; but the amount is immaterial. For the returns for 1896, see Appendix II.

CHAPTER XIV.

THE APPROXIMATE LIMIT OF DEEP MINING.

PHYSICAL IMPEDIMENTS.

WE have now completed the statistical part of our enquiry, and have found that approximately there will remain at the close of this century a quantity of coal available for future use amounting to nearly EIGHTY-TWO THOUSAND MILLIONS OF TONS down to a depth of 4000 feet from the surface. This quantity divided by the estimated output at the same period, namely, two hundred millions of tons, will be sufficient to last for a little over four hundred years. This duration will doubtless be entirely satisfactory to the present generation when regarded as a whole; but when tested by individual districts may appear otherwise.

If we revert to a period not so distant, namely, the year 1860, when I estimated the available quantity of unworked coal, and measured it by the then rate of consumption, we are met by a very different result. At that time, having estimated the quantity at nearly eighty thousand millions of tons, I was able to assert that, at the *then* rate of production, this would suffice to give a supply for nearly one thousand years.* The estimates of the Commissioners largely increased those arrived at by myself, and are adopted with modifications in this work; but now it will be observed that the period of duration, based on a revised summary of the Royal Commission only amounts to about four hundred years, on the supposition that the drain remains stationary at the quantity estimated to be raised at the close of the century. The increase of production has, therefore, been more than sufficient to compensate for the increased estimates of the Commissioners as compared with those determined ten years previously by myself, and the period is reduced by considerably more than one-half.

But, having regard to past experience, who can venture to affirm that the output of coal in the twentieth century will remain at the figure above indicated? Since the year 1854, when we were for the first time supplied with reliable statements regarding the amount of the annual output,† the amount has increased threefold; namely, from 64,661,401 to 189,574,311 tons in 1895; in other words, there has been an annual increase at the rate of over three millions of tons, notwithstanding occasional checks such as occurred in the year 1893,

---

* The output in 1860 amounted to 84,042,698 tons.

† By the publication of 'The Mineral Statistics of Great Britain,' collected by the late Mr. Robert Hunt, F.R.S.

owing to the prolonged strike in the Midlands. A continuously increasing drain in the next century, in any degree corresponding to that of the century now drawing to a close, would result in an alarming diminution of the coal-resources of the British Isles, in a migration of existing industrial communities from present centres of manufacturing industry to others, and in a general falling off in the commerce of the whole kingdom.

It may, however, be objected that I have adopted an arbitrary limit for the depth at which coal may be wrought by assuming 4000 feet from the surface as such a limit; and it may be pointed out that there are admittedly seams of coal extending to depths much greater than this; as, for example, in Cheshire, Yorkshire and South Wales. The reply is a perfectly fair one, and it is right that I should give some reasons why this question of depth has been adopted in the above sense.

I may first observe that the limit of approximately 4000 feet was adopted not only by myself in 1860, but by the Commissioners ten years later, after a most exhaustive discussion of the question; so that on this point we are entirely at one. It was also adopted by Lord Armstrong in his Presidential Address to the British Association at Newcastle-upon-Tyne in 1860, as also by Professor W. Stanley Jevons in his well-known treatise.* This general concurrence will probably suffice to prove that

* 'The Coal Question' (1865).

there are good grounds for the course which has been adopted in these pages; but in addition it may be as well to quote the statement of one of the chief Inspectors of Mines for the "Midland" districts, which embraces, not only Leicestershire and Warwickshire, but also Nottinghamshire and Derbyshire. Mr. A. H. Stokes, in his annual report for 1889, observes that in that district coal has not yet been worked below one-half the depth fixed as the limit to which coal might be *practically* worked, and he shows that at that date the greatest depth of coal-mining (measured by the depth of the shafts) was for Derbyshire, 1700 feet; for Leicestershire, 1100 feet; for Nottinghamshire, 1700 feet; and for Warwickshire, 1100 feet.* The depths may have slightly increased since; and in other districts, such as Lancashire and Cheshire, coal is worked at still greater depths, while we may feel assured that in the earlier part of the Twentieth Century there will be many shafts penetrating the crust to depths of 3000 feet and upwards.

The impediments to coal-mining at excessive depths fall under two heads: those of an economic or mechanical character, and those due to physical or natural causes. Under the former head is to be included the increased expense required, not only in sinking the shafts, of which a pair are required by Act of Parliament, but on account of

* Report of H.M. Inspector of Mines for 1889, p. 11.

the calibre of the machinery and plant used for winding the coal. Time is also an element of cost, as it is necessary for the owners to wait for several years before their capital can produce any fair return. A large and deep colliery may require an outlay of 100,000*l.* or more, and it may take three or four years to sink the shafts, to set up the machinery and to open out the coal itself, so as to bring to the surface and send to market a quantity which will yield a fair return upon the capital expended.

1. *Temperature of Mines.*—Amongst the physical obstacles which increase with the depth, there are two which may be referred to here, as being inevitable ; namely, increase of temperature in the strata themselves, and therefore in the air which circulates in the passages of the mine, and increase of pressure due to the weight of the superincumbent strata. This latter obstacle, however, is capable of being overcome to a great extent, especially under the "long-wall" system of mining. I shall, therefore, pass it over in order to discuss the question of increase of temperature, which is of greater urgency.

That the temperature of the crust everywhere increases as we descend from a point a few feet below the surface, where the temperature is invariable all the year round, is a fact that has been abundantly demonstrated by experiments carried out at intervals all over the globe—and to depths exceeding 4000 feet from the surface. I shall here present the reader with some of the more important of these observations and results.*

2. *Dukinfield Colliery.*—The experiments carried out by Mr. Astley, during the progress of sinking the Dukinfield Colliery, are perhaps the most valuable of any hitherto undertaken in this country. Through the kindness of the late Dr. Fairbairn, of Manchester, I have been supplied with the whole of the details, which I here insert at length. The observations were conducted with great care. The thermometer was inserted in a dry bore-hole, and removed as far as possible from the influence of the air in the shaft, and left in its bed for a length of time, varying from half an hour to two hours. The results also carry with them more than usual importance, from the fact that they extend downwards to a depth of 2055 feet, with an additional observation made in the open workings, at 120 yards from the shaft, and at a depth of 2151 feet.

The first observation gives $51°$ as the invariable temperature throughout the year at a depth of $15\frac{1}{2}$ feet.† Between 231 yards and 270 yards, the temperature was nearly uniform at $58·0$, and the

---

* Most of these are contained in the two last editions of 'The Coal-fields of Great Britain.' The temperatures are on the Fahrenheit scale.

† This observation for the position of the invariable stratum is probably not reliable. The depth ought to be greater, but its accurate determination requires a series of observations which could not well have been made in the present instance.

THERMOMETRICAL OBSERVATIONS IN THE DUKINFIELD COLLIERY, CHESHIRE, BETWEEN 1848 AND 1859.

Date.	Depth in Yards.	Temperature Fahr.	Description of Stratum.
1848.		°	
July 28th	5·6	51	Bed rock—no variation
1849.			
1st	231	57·7	Blue shale—wet
12th	234·7	58	,, dry hole
16th	237	58	,, ,,
July 14th	239	57·5	,, ,,
,, 16th	240	58	,, ,,
,, 27th	242	57·5	,, ,,
Aug. 9th	244	58	,, ,,
,, 25th	248	58	,, water
,, 27th	248	57·25	,, ,,
,, 31st	250	57·25	,, ,,
Nov. 14th	252	58	
Dec. 6th	256·5	58	,, dry
,, 15th	262·5	58·5	,, ,,
,, 22nd	270	58	Bituminous shale—dry
1850.			
Jan. 9th	279	58·5	Strong warrant earth
,, 26th	286·5	59·12	Rock bands
Feb. 11th	293	59·5	Coal roof
,, 19th	300	59·87	Warrant earth
March 5th	309	59·87	Purple mottled shale
1851.			
June 9th	358	62·5	Warrant earth
Aug. 14th	373	64	Tender blue shale
Nov. 7th	403	65	Coal roof
,, 19th	419	65·37	Rock bands

* These observations are published by Dr. Fairbairn, F.R.S., in the Report of the British Association for 1861.

THERMOMETRICAL OBSERVATIONS, ETC.—*continued*.

Date.	Depth in Yards.	Temperature Fahr.	Description of Stratum.
1852.		°	
Feb. 6th	433	66·5	Black shale
May 28th	446	67	Strong fire-clay
1857.			
Feb. 28th	483·5	67·25	Sandstone—dry hole
March 7th	487	67·76	Shale
April 11th	501	68·5	Sandstone
May 6th	511·5	68·75	Blue shale
,, 19th	521·5	69·38	Strong shale
June 9th	533	69·75	Warrant earth
,, 22nd	539	69·88	Blue shale
,, 27th	546	71·75	Coal and earth
July 18th	555	71·25	Grey sandstone
Aug. 1st	563	72·25	Red rock (sandstone)
,, 15th	569	71·25	,, wet hole
Sept. 2nd	578	72·12	,, ,,
,, 19th	589	71·5	,, ,,
Oct. 3rd	597	72·25	Grey rock—dry hole
,, 17th	608	72·25	Coal roof—wet hole
,, 27th	613·5	72·25	Coal floor ,,
1858.			
March 22nd	621	72	Strong shale—dry
,, 29th	627	71·5	Dark-blue shale
April 23rd	645·5	72·25	Shale—dry hole
May 1st	651	72·25	,,
,, 19th	658	72·5	,,
June 9th	669	73·25	Bituminous shale—dry hole
,, 19th	673	74·12	Grey rock
July 17th	683	75·25	Blue shale
,, 21st	685	75·5	,,
1859.			
March 5th *	717	75·0	" Black Mine " coal roof

* In workings at 120 yards down engine incline from the shaft.

increase from the surface would be at the rate of 1° Fahr. for 88 feet.

2. Between 270 and 309 yards, the increase was at the rate of 1° for 62·4 feet.

3. Between 309 and 419 yards, the increase was at the rate 1° for 60 feet.

4. Between 419 and 613 yards, the increase was at the rate of 1° for 86·91 feet.

5. Between 613 and 685 yards, the increase was at the rate of 1° for 65·6 feet.

6. The last observation, taken in the mine itself, at 120 yards from the pit, is valuable, as showing that the temperature of the air does not greatly differ from that of the surrounding strata.

The result of the whole series of observations (making allowance for the doubt regarding the first observation) gives an increase of about 1° for every 80 feet, which is a less rapid increase than that exhibited by the generality of experiments. But before discussing the cause of this abnormally slow rate of increase I wish the reader to become acquainted with the experiments of not less interest and value made at another colliery near Wigan, and extending to a still greater depth, and in the same parallel of latitude.

3. *Rose Bridge Colliery, Wigan.*—The following observations on the temperature of the strata during the progress of sinking the pits of Rose Bridge Colliery, at Ince, near Wigan, one of the deepest

mines in Britain, have been communicated to the author by Mr. Bryham, the Manager, by whom they were carried out. They differ materially from those of Dukinfield just described.*

THERMOMETRICAL OBSERVATIONS AT ROSE BRIDGE COLLIERY.

Date.	Depth in Yards.	Strata.	Temperature in Open Pit.	Temperature in Solid Strata.
			° F.	° F.
July, 1854	161	Blue shale	..	64·5
August, 1854	188	Warrant earth	..	66
May, 1858	550	Blue shale	..	78
July, 1858	600	Warrant earth	..	80
May 18, 1868	630	"Raven" coal	73	83
July 24, 1868	665	Strong shale	75	85
April 19, 1869	673	"Yard Coal" mine	76	86
Nov. 18, 1868	700	Strong blue metal	76	87
Feb. 22, 1869	736	Ditto	76	88½
March 12, 1869	748	Shale	77	89
April 17, 1869	762	Linn and wool, or strong shale	78	90·5
May 3, 1869	774	Strong shale	80	91·5
May 19, 1869	782	Blue metal	79	92
July 8, 1869	801	Strong blue shale	79	93
July 16, 1869	808	Coal (Arley mine)	79	93½

* These observations, with a complete section of the strata to a depth of 815 yards from the surface, are given in the 'Third Report of the Committee on Underground Temperature,' Rep. Brit. Assoc., 1870.

Assuming the surface temperature to be 49°, we have on the whole depth of 808 yards, or 2424 feet, an increase of 44·5°, which is at the rate of ·0184 of a degree per foot, or one degree for every 54·4 feet, as against one degree for every 80 feet at Dukinfield. This difference calls for some explanation.

4. *Cause of Difference in Rate of Increase.*—With strata so nearly similar, and in two neighbouring counties, we should scarcely have expected so much difference in the mean rates of increase downwards. In this respect Rose Bridge agrees nearly with the average results obtained elsewhere; Dukinfield far surpasses all other deep mines or wells, so far as our present records extend, in slowness of increase.*

In a paper published in the 'Proceedings of the Royal Society of London,'† I have endeavoured to show that the cause of the discrepancy in the results obtained at the two localities is due to the differences in the position of the strata in each case. At Rose Bridge the beds are nearly horizontal, at Dukinfield they are inclined at an angle varying from 30° to 35°, rising and cropping out to the eastward. Now, strata of various kinds, such as alternating sandstones, shales, clays, and coal, with different conducting powers, must offer more resistance to the transmission of heat in a direction across, than when parallel to, their planes of bedding; for Mr. Hopkins

* *Ibid.*, p. 32.
† Proc. Royal Society, 1870, vol. xviii. p. 175.

has shown, that every sudden change of material is equivalent to an increase of resistance. And it is obvious that highly-inclined strata, such as those at Dukinfield, furnish a path by which internal heat can travel obliquely upwards and outwards, without being interrupted by these breaches of continuity. On the other hand, deep-seated horizontal strata, like those of Rose Bridge, offer a succession of resisting surfaces to the upward passage of internal heat.

As, therefore, the rate of increase of temperature is inversely proportional to the upward flow of the heat, we have here a solution of the results arrived at in the cases before us. To this it may be added, that inclined strata furnish great facilities for the convection of heat by the flow of water along the planes of junction.

The general inference which may be drawn from the cases just described, as far as they bear upon the temperature of coal-mines, is this: that in those districts where the strata are highly inclined (at angles varying from 30°—60°), the underground temperature will be lower than in the case of those where the strata are in a position approaching the horizontal.

5. *Mean Result.*—The illustrations already adduced will probably be considered sufficient to show that the increase of temperature is a reality, which becomes a sensible obstacle at a slightly variable

depth; and will have to be encountered and overcome by artificial means when the depth exceeds 800 or 900 yards. On this point the Commissioners on Coal Resources have arrived at the conclusion that at a depth of 1000 yards (3000 feet) the temperature of the earth would amount to 98°. Under "the long-wall system" of working, a difference of about 7° appears to exist between the temperature of the air and that of the working faces, and this difference represents a further depth of 420 feet; so that the depth at which the temperature of the air would, under the present conditions, become equal to the heat of the blood, would be about 3420 feet. Beyond this point the considerations affecting increase of depth become so speculative, that the Commissioners leave them in uncertainty; but they consider it may be fairly assumed that a depth of at least 4000 feet may ultimately be reached in coal-mining.*

In reviewing the evidence laid before them by several gentlemen of experience, the Commissioners have come to the conclusion that the rate of increase may, for ordinary cases, be assumed to be 1° Fahr. for every 60 feet. From this mean result there will be variations, as in the case of Dukinfield and Rose Bridge; one of which gives a less rapid, the other a more rapid, rate of increase. Assuming, however,

* Report, vol. i. p. 88.

the rate as above stated, it is necessary to determine the temperature to which the addition of 1° for 60 feet is to be made, in order to calculate the temperature at different depths; in other words, the position of the "*invariable stratum.*"

Now, it has been found that at a certain depth, varying from 30 to 50 feet, the temperature remains the same all the year round; and is nearly that of the mean annual temperature of the place. The depth of this "invariable stratum" according to Humboldt, depends upon the latitude of the place (increasing from the equator towards the poles), on the conducting power of the rock, and on the amount of difference between the temperatures of the hottest and coldest seasons. At Greenwich, the mean temperature is 49·5°; and in the deepest of several underground thermometers, 25 feet from the surface, the extreme variations were (1858) from 48·85° to 52·27°, giving a mean of 50·56°—a result, differing by only half a degree from that of Dukinfield Colliery, obtained ten years earlier.*

We may therefore adopt 50·5° as the standard of departure—or, in other words, the *temperature of no variation* at a depth of about 50 feet underground.

But there is an additional element tending to raise the heat in deep mines, namely, the increased density of the air. The effect of this will be greatest when the air is stagnant; but when there is a rapid

* "Greenwich Observations" for 1858.

circulation of the air-current, it will probably be small, and may be disregarded.*

The following Table gives the maximum temperature at the various depths according to the average rate of 1° Fahr. for 60 feet :—

TABLE SHOWING THEORETICAL INCREASE OF TEMPERATURE.

Depth in Feet.	Increase of Temperature due to Depth.	Depth in Feet.	Increase of Temperature due to Depth.
	° F.		° F.
1000	63·0	2750	95·5
1500	73·8	3000	99·6
1750	78·8	3250	103·8
2000	82·0	3500	108·0
2250	87·1	3750	112·1
2500	91·3	4000	116·3

From the above Table it will be observed that at a depth of 3000 feet the temperature of the strata exceeds that of blood heat, and that were it not for the effects of ventilation in reducing the temperature, the limits of coal-mining would be circumscribed within this depth.†

* This element has not been noticed by the Commissioners, though I drew attention to it in the second edition of this work. From this I infer that the Commissioners did not consider the increased density of the air in a well-ventilated mine as calculated materially to increase the temperature.

† Professor Prestwich has adopted 49·5° Fahr. as the thermometrical gradient for coal-mines, in which case the rate of increase

6. *Ventilation.*—To effective ventilation, however, we must look for ability to win those seams which lie within the additional thousand feet of strata; and as to what extent this is likely to be accomplished, we have already some valuable evidence. In reference to the effect of the heated walls of the rock on the ventilating air-current, the Commissioners remark as follows *:—When cool air enters a heated mine it absorbs heat from the surfaces of the passages through which it flows, and the rate of this absorption somewhat exceeds the ratio of the difference between the temperature of the air and that of the surrounding surface with which it is in contact. By the absorption which thus takes place the air is heated, and this heating process is most rapid at first, when the difference of temperature is greatest, and gradually diminishes as the length of the passage is extended, never ceasing until complete assimilation of the temperature is effected. The progress towards assimilation is more rapid when the air comes in contact with the working face of the coal, which, from being newly exposed, is more highly heated than the surfaces of the permanent air courses. The rapidity, however, with which the air takes up the heat from the working face depends in

would be more rapid than that given in the Table above, Proc. Roy. Soc., Feb. 12, 1885, p. 54.

* Report, vol. i. p. 82 (Committee A, of which Sir W. C. Armstrong, C.B., was chairman).

a great degree upon the system of working. In the cellular system, called "pillar and stall," the air seems to acquire almost immediately the full temperature of the coal; but under the "long-wall" system there are instances of the air retaining a considerable inferiority of temperature after sweeping past the working face.

7. *Temperature of Air-Current.*—The experiments made by Mr. Bryham, the Manager of Rose Bridge Colliery, near Wigan, for the purpose of determining the rate of increase of temperature of the air-current while flowing through the passages of a deep mine, are of much interest. They are taken at the respective depths of 300 and 600 yards, and at different periods of the year, and are as follows:—

OBSERVATIONS ON TEMPERATURES OF AIR-CURRENTS, ETC., AT ROSE BRIDGE COLLIERY, WIGAN.

Temperature at Surface in Shade, 56°.

Date.	Depth in Yards.	Air Current. Cubic ft. per min.	Temperature of Intake Air.	Temperature of Return Air.	Gain of Heat.	Distance travelled by the Current.
1860. Sept. 4	300	35·00	59·5	64·0	5·5	1000 yards.
,,	..	..	..	68·0	8·5	4 yards out of air-current.
,,	600	81·76	60·5	73·0	12·5	1500 yards.
,,	..	..	..	75·0	15·0	8 yards out of current.

Temperature at Surface in Shade, 42°.

Date.	Depth in Yards.	Air Current. Cubic ft. per min.	Temperature of Intake Air.	Temperature of Return Air.	Gain of Heat.	Distance travelled by the Current.
1861. Mar. 18	600	105·58	50·75	..	..	Main intake.
,,	..	96·40	..	68·75	18·0	Taken in Dumb Drift; distance travelled, 2200 yards.
,,	..	23·26	51·5	67·5	16·0	Distance travelled, 2400 yards.
,,	..	31·50	51·0	..	..	
,,	..	21·00	..	71·0	20·0	Distance travelled, 3140 yards.
,,	..	10·50	..	67·5	16·5	Distance travelled, 1900 yards.
,,	..	..	60·0	..	..	4 yards out of main intake air.
,,	..	..	..	71·75	11·75	4 yards out of main return air.

Barometer in Cannel Mine (600 yards) 30·5, at surface 28·8.

The above experiments bring out many points of interest. 1. We cannot but be struck with the enormous amount of caloric continually being carried off from the mine. Thus, in one of the experiments, it is shown that at a depth of 600 yards a current of air equal to 21 cubic feet per minute passes off from the mine 20° warmer than when it entered, after circulating through 3140 yards. 2. It will be observed that the surface temperature, depending upon the season of the year, materially affects the temperature of the whole mine; and if the extreme temperatures of summer and winter had been observed, the results would doubtless have been proportionate. Thus, with a surface temperature of 56°, the return air is 73° with 1500 yards of circulation, while with a surface temperature of 42° the return air is only 67·5° with 1900 yards. 3. The increase of heat received by the air while passing down the shaft appears to be considerable. Thus, in a depth of 300 yards the increase was $59·5 - 56 = 3·5°$; and in a depth of 600 yards the increase was $60·5 - 56 = 4·5°$ in September, and $50·75 - 42 = 8·75°$ in March. Lastly: several observations show how powerful is the air-current in moderating the temperature; for whenever the thermometer was placed beyond its influence, the mercury immediately ascended. All these points bear directly upon the question of the limits of deep mining.

8. *Effects of the Seasons.*—It might have been supposed that the influence of the comparatively colder air of winter and warmer air of summer would be felt throughout the workings of a coal-mine, but the Commissioners have come to a different conclusion, upon the evidence offered them on this subject. All the witnesses examined agreed in stating that summer and winter make no difference in the temperature of the air in mines, except at short distances from the shaft. This is due to the fact that great disparity of temperature is rapidly reduced when the air comes in contact with the air

passages. Thus, very cold air upon entering the mine rapidly absorbs the heat of the strata, and the greater the difference of temperature the more rapid is the absorption. I am, therefore, induced to abandon an opinion which I formerly held, that air at a low winter temperature might be, in some cases, rendered available for mines which in the summer months might become unworkable.

9. *Effect of the Increased Circulation of Air-Current.*— On this subject, the evidence offered chiefly by Mr. Lindsay Wood, of Hetton Hall; Mr. J. J. Atkinson, of Chilton Moor; and Mr. John Knowles, of Pendlebury, has tended to show that little change of temperature is effected by increasing the circulation of the air in the passages of the mine. From the tabulated statement given in the report, it appears that in one case observed at Hetton Collieries, when the distance from the shaft was from 2296 to 2925 yards, the difference between temperature of strata and of the air was only 2°, while the volume of air in circulation was 22,400 cubic feet per minute in one case, and 11,400 in another.

Mr. Wood has shown by a table the gradual approximation of the temperature of the air to that of the strata through a distance of 3422 yards; and he found that at that distance no perceptible difference took place in the temperature of the current when reduced from 41,800 cubic feet to 3000 per minute.

10. *Effect of Humidity or Dryness of the Air.*— The question of the maximum temperature of air

which is compatible with healthful labour is an exceedingly difficult one to determine, and the Commissioners had evidence laid before them showing that in some cases human labour had been carried on at temperatures as high as 180° Fahr.; but it was observed that in these cases the thermometer indicated radiant heat, and not that of the surrounding air. Upon one question, however, the witnesses were unanimous: that a high temperature was endurable very much in proportion to the dryness of the air; while on the other hand, where it was saturated with moisture, the same degree of temperature became intolerable.

Now, it is a matter of general observation that in deep mines the air is comparatively dry. The water, which is generally present, often in large quantities in shallow mines, gradually lessens in quantity as we descend, and at depths of 500 or 600 yards ceases altogether. The air, therefore, which circulates through the passages of deep mines gradually parts with its moisture while it rises in temperature, and passes into a state agreeable to the human system and conducive to health. The hygrometric condition of the air in deep mines may, therefore, be regarded as in some measure tending to counterbalance the effects of a high temperature, and to render possible healthful labour at great depths from the surface.

The above experiments will probably suffice to give the reader a general idea regarding the effect of the increase of temperature of the strata as we descend upon the air-current which circulates through the mine; and which serves not only to supply air to the miners, but to carry off the gases which to a greater or less degree are everywhere present. Experience will probably be necessary in order to determine with any approach to certainty the limit of depth of working in coal-mines due to the temperature of the air. We may feel certain, however, that with the ever-inceasing depths of the shafts and accompanying expense, the distance to which seams of coal will be worked from the bottom of the shaft will be increased, and the difficulty of reducing the temperature will increase proportionately. INCREASE is the principle which everywhere suggests itself as we contemplate the future of mining. Increase in depth; increase in magnitude of plant and machinery; increase in extent of underground works; increase in rate of delivery of coal at the surface; increase of ventilation; increase of expense in every direction; and increase in the price of the coal itself.

11. *Effects of Pressure.*—We are unable to speak with certainty regarding the effect of the pressure on the strata at great depths as an impediment to mining. That the effects in regard to crushing, on the extraction of the coal, are considerable we know from experience in deep mines; but it may be presumed that the obstacle is one capable of being overcome by mechanical appliances.

CHAPTER XV.

PROGRESSIVE AND RETROGRESSIVE MINING DISTRICTS.

AMONGST the different coal-producing districts there is of course great disparity as regards resources, not only in regard to area and thickness of the seams of coal, but also as regards limits of depth. While some of our coal-fields extend to depths from the surface of 4000 feet and more, others are limited to a depth of about 3000 feet. Amongst the former we may especially mention the coal-basins of South Wales, and of Somersetshire; the coal-fields of Lancashire and Cheshire, of Yorkshire, Derbyshire, and Nottinghamshire, and of North Staffordshire. Amongst the latter may be named the coal-fields of the Scottish group; of Cumberland, of Durham and Northumberland; of Leicestershire, Warwickshire; South Staffordshire; of Shropshire and of the Forest of Dean; in all constituting the majority amongst the coal-producing areas of the British Isles.* For these the limit of depth is already settled by the limits of their own

* Those of Ireland come under the latter head.

K

form and structure; so that the question regarding the possible limits of depth for coal-mines only applies to about a moiety of the total coal-producing areas. The life (so to speak) of the latter class will in the ordinary course of events be less prolonged than that of the former, and already signs of exhaustion are visible in the case of several districts.

With some exceptions, depending on the quality of the coal and local demand, the character of any coal-producing area may be determined by the increase or decrease in the production of the mineral. Thus we may classify these areas into progressive, stationary, and retrogressive; and in the last case this character is a certain sign of approaching exhaustion. Taking these characters in the order named, we find them ranging themselves as follows :—

1. *Progressive Coal-Areas.*—1. South Wales and Monmouthshire; 2. North Midland district, including Yorkshire, Derbyshire, and Nottinghamshire; 3. Scottish group; 4. Lancashire and Cheshire group; 5. Great Northern district of Northumberland and Durham; 6. Denbighshire; 7. Warwickshire; 8. Cumberland (slightly); 9. Leicestershire (slightly).

2. *Stationary Coal-Areas.*—1. Bristol and Somersetshire; 2. Forest of Dean.

3. *Retrogressive Coal-Areas.*—1. South Staffordshire; 2. Flintshire; and 3. Coalbrook Dale (Salop).

The above classification may be taken as a criterion of resource; the "retrogressive" areas are fast approaching exhaustion; but of those on the "progressive" list, some, by the magnitude of their annual output as compared with their storage, are also fast reducing their length of "life"; and of these the "Great Northern" coal-field, the seat of which is at Newcastle-on-Tyne, and which is historically the most interesting of all the coal-producing areas of the British Isles, is surely and rapidly exhausting its strength.

This is a matter which cannot fail to have an important influence on the great manufacturing industries of this district during the incoming century. The process of depletion is less rapid to the east and south of the Wear and Tyne, than in opposite directions towards the outcrop of the coal-seams; and supplies will continue to be drawn from the former tracts after they have ceased in the latter.

CHAPTER XVI.

FOREIGN COAL-FIELDS.

It is not a part of the design of this work to go into a detailed description of the coal-fields outside the British Islands; but a short *excursus* into foreign parts may not be an unfitting conclusion to the subject in hand. The "Statement" issued by the Board of Trade, dated August 1894, and founded on an Order of the House of Commons, gives us the results of enquiries made into the coal-production and consumption in countries not under the Crown, and is of much interest. The returns range from 1883 to 1893 inclusive, but I shall limit my reference to the later date. In all cases there is increase in the output between the two periods, and accompanying the "Statement" of the quantities raised is a table showing the value in English money of the quantities raised "at the pit mouth," as well as the average value of coal per ton in each country. The countries referred to are: (1) The Russian Empire, (2) Sweden, (3) Germany, (4) Belgium, (5) France, (6) Spain, (7) Austria-Hungary, (8) Italy, (9) Japan, and (10) the United States of America; we shall consider them in the order above named.

I. COUNTRIES NOT UNDER THE BRITISH CROWN.

(1) *The Russian Empire.*—The quantity raised in this vast region is chiefly derived from the coal-fields of Central Russia, the basin of the Donetz in Southern Russia, the basin of the Kousnetsk in the Altai and the Oural range; that of the Donetz is the most important.* The output (1893) amounted only to 7,535,000 metric tons, and is about double that of 1883. Russia is now developing the petroleum wells which are sunk in a band of country along the northern base of the Caucasus, and is making use of this liquid fuel to a large extent for machinery and locomotive engines.

(2) *Sweden.*—The amount of coal (or lignite) raised in this country amounted in 1894 to only 214,000 tons.

(3) *Germany.*—This is the most important coal-producing country on the European continent, and yet the quantity of coal raised does not reach to one-half of that produced in Great Britain. Coalfields occur in the Rhenish provinces of Prussia (Saarbrück), in Saxony, in Zwickau-Chemnitz, and Plauenscher Grund, Westphalia, Ibbenbüren and Piesberg in Hanover, Moravia and Silesia. The quantity of coal raised in 1894 was 76,741,000 tons,

---

* 'Coal-fields of Great Britain,' 4th edition, p. 382. For further information regarding the coal-fields here described, the reader is referred to the above work.

of the value of 25,455,000*l*. In 1883, the quantity raised was 55,943,000 tons.

(4) *Belgium.*—The coal-formation of this country stretches along an E. and W. trough from Aix-la-Chapelle, by Liége and Namur to the frontiers of France. It is to a large extent concealed under newer formations of Cretaceous and Tertiary age. The quantity of coal raised in 1894 amounted to 20,534,000 tons, of the value of 7,652,000*l*.

(5) *France.*—This country comes next to Germany in its coal-production, but by a long distance behind. The formation is the western portion of the Belgian Carboniferous trough, which is now known to stretch from Calais under the Straits to Dover. The output in 1894 was 26,964,000 tons, of the value of about 12,150,000*l*.

(6) *Spain.*—This country has valuable coal-fields in Asturias and in the province of Ternel and Castellon de la Plana, but the amount of coal produced is small, amounting in 1894 to 1,657,000 tons.

(7) *Austria-Hungary.*—Coal-fields are found in Eastern Moravia, along the banks of the Oder, Rossitz and Oslawan; in Hungary at Oravitza, Eibenthal on the Lower Danube, and at Gran. The quantity turned out in 1893, amounted to 10,716,000 tons, of the value of 3,226,000*l*.

(8) *Italy.*—This country is not fortunate in the possession of coal resources of any great importance; her only possessions are some anthracite

beds on the flanks of the Western Alps, producing 317,000 tons in 1893. Lignite occurs in small quantities.

(9) *Japan.*—The development of the coal resources of this country is making rapid strides. In 1883, the output of coal amounted to 1,021,000 tons, but in 1893 it reached 3,371,000 tons. The mines are worked in the districts of Kiusiu and Niphon, while there are supposed to be considerable stores of mineral fuel in the islands of Formosa and Karapty.*

(10) *United States.*—The vast extent of the Carboniferous strata with coal is now well known, and the mineral is being rapidly developed so as at this time to fall little short of the output of the British Isles. In 1883 the output amounted to 102,863,000 tons; but in 1893 it had reached 162,815,000 tons, very little short of that raised in this country.† That year, however, witnessed the disastrous strike of the Midlands, so that the output was about twenty millions of tons lower than it would have been under normal conditions of trade. Some of the best steam coal in the world is drawn from the "Poccahontas" mines, and is shipped at the terminus of the railway at Norfolk. The resources of the United States coal-fields are doubtless enormous, surpassing those of the United Kingdom at the present day. They have a superficial area of about 229,000 square

---

* See Curzon's 'Problems of the Far East,' p. 52.
† In 1894, the output only amounted to 152,448,000 tons.

miles, and occupy portions of the New England States, Pennsylvania, Maryland, West Virginia, Ohio, East Kentucky, Tennessee, Georgia and Alabama. They also form portions of Illinois, Indiana, Missouri, Arkansas and Texas.

II. COUNTRIES UNDER THE BRITISH CROWN.

Referring the reader to my former work for descriptions of the coal-fields of these countries, I will here content myself with giving the returns issued by the Board of Trade.*

(1) *British India.*—The output has been steadily advancing since 1883, when the quantity raised amounted to 1,315,976 tons; in 1894, the output reached 2,820,652 tons; while the number of persons employed was 43,197, being 65 tons for each person annually. The average value of a ton of coal at the pit mouth was 4s. 0½d. The coal-fields are situated in Bengal, Orissa, the Central Provinces, Sikkim and Assam.†

(2) *Canada.*—The coal-fields are chiefly situated in Nova Scotia, and the output has been slowly increasing since 1883, when it reached 1,806,259 tons; in 1894, the output was 3,867,742 tons.

---

* Dated September 3, 1895, and signed by Mr. Courtenay Boyle; also 'Mineral Statistics' for the year 1895, issued by the Home Office, 1896.

† 'Coal-fields of Great Britain,' 4th edition, p. 394.

(3) *New South Wales.*—The coal-fields of this colony are of great extent and value, and the output is steadily increasing. In 1883 it amounted to 2,521,457 tons; and in 1894, to 3,672,076 tons. At Cremorne Point in Sydney Harbour a large colliery is being put down to work the well-known "Metropolitan" or "Bulli" seam, of 10 feet in thickness in the centre of the coal-basin, and at a depth of 2929 feet from the surface; the depth of the seam was determined by boring in 1893.

(4) *Victoria*—The output from this colony is small, only reaching 171,660 tons in 1894.

(5) *Queensland.*—The output was 270,705 tons in 1894.

(6) *Tasmania.*—The output was 30,922 tons in 1894.

(7) *New Zealand.*—The coal-fields of this country are locally extensive, but only partially developed. The output in 1894 amounted to 719,546 tons.*

(8) *Cape of Good Hope.*—The output was 69,690 tons in 1894.

(9) *Natal.*—The output was 138,610 tons in 1894.

There are other countries, such as China, largely stored with coal, where coal-mining is only in its infancy. Western ideas must gain ascendency before mining can be carried on to a beneficial extent.

* A very full account of these will be found in Trans. Fed. Inst. Mining Engineers, by George J. Binns, vol. xii. (1896).

Coal-mining and railway communication must go hand in hand, and at present the Chinese have a great repugnance to seeing land, which may contain the bones of their ancestors, being disturbed and traversed by locomotives.

III. THE AVERAGE VALUE OF COAL AT THE PIT'S MOUTH IN VARIOUS COUNTRIES.

Amongst the interesting particulars brought to light by the "Returns" published by the Board of Trade, and collected by Mr. Courtenay Boyle,* is the average value of the coal produced in various countries taken as "at the pit's mouth" and given in English money; from which it is gratifying to observe that, with the exception of the United States of America, the price of coal is less in Great Britain than in any country to which the returns refer. In Germany, however, it is only slightly higher, but in France and Belgium the prices are much in excess of those of the former countries. This is probably due to the extreme physical difficulties, involving increased cost, to which coal-mining is subject in France and Belguim as compared with either Britain or Germany. In America much of the coal is extracted in the least expensive of all ways; namely, by driving adits into the hill-sides, and thus avoiding the cost of pits and machinery.

* Dated September 3, 1895; edited by Sir R. Giffen.

This mode of mining is that adopted in countries where new fields are being opened up, but it becomes less and less available where mining has been in progress for lengthened periods.

AVERAGE PRICES OF COAL AT THE PIT'S MOUTH.

Country.	1892.	1893.	1894.	1895.
	s. d.	s. d.	s. d.	s. d.
United States	6 3	6 3	5 3¼	5 3¼
Great Britain	7 3½	6 9½	6 8	6 1¾
Germany	7 4½	6 9	6 7½	,,
France	9 11½	9 2¾	9 0¼	,,
Belgium	8 2¾	7 5¾	7 5½	,,
Spain	4 6¾	4 6¾	5 9¼	,,
Austria (lignite)	3 1¼	3 4½	,,	,,
Hungary ,,	5 3¼	5 4½	,,	,,

From the same source we learn that the average value of coal produced in the British colonies has been in past years far higher than in the mother country. Thus, in New South Wales the average value from 1883 to 1888 was over 9s. per ton, but in 1894 the average had fallen to 6s. 4d. per ton, or very much the same as in the United Kingdom. The average value of coal in New Zealand, namely, 11s. per ton, continues comparatively high, and the same remark applies to that in Canada, where the average value in 1894 was 9s. per ton. In

British India the value of coal ranges low; in 1894 it amounted to 4s. 0½d. per ton.

IV. Percentage of Coal consumed in Foreign Countries.

Another matter of interest dealt with in these Returns is that showing the percentages of coal consumed in various foreign countries, whether of native production, or of British or any other origin. In the United Kingdom, practically the whole of the coal consumed, as might have been expected, is of native production. The same is the case with the United States, Germany, and to a less extent with Belgium and France.

Russia consumes, roughly speaking, 79 per cent. of native production, 17 per cent. of British coal, and 4 per cent. from other countries. Sweden draws upon us for 88 per cent. of her coal; France requires 12 per cent. of British, and 17 per cent. of other coal. In Spain the coal consumed is about half of native, and half of British, origin: whilst in Italy almost the whole of the coal consumed is of British origin. These tables ought to be studied, in order to impress the reader with the view to how large an extent, though of course in a very minor degree as compared with local resources, foreign countries depend upon the British Isles for their necessary supplies of mineral fuel.

CHAPTER XVII.

A FORECAST.

I DO not claim the power of forecasting the future; but were I to indulge in a practice sometimes attempted by statesmen and writers, it would not be for the purpose of conjuring up the vision of Macaulay's New Zealander surveying the ruins of the metropolis of the empire from London Bridge. The loss or serious diminution of our coal supplies may materially affect the character and habits of our people, but does not necessarily imply the descent of Great Britain from the high position she occupies amongst the nations of the world. All history teaches us that the greatness of any country depends only in a minor degree on physical advantages. The cases of Holland on the one hand, and of Spain on the other, are apposite illustrations of this truth. Spain, once paramount in both hemispheres and mistress of the sea, is now reduced to the position of a second-rate power, destitute of influence, stript of her dependencies, and still undergoing the process of depletion; yet her mineral wealth and her natural position give her enormous advantages in the competition for power amongst the nations. On the other hand, Holland, a small state destitute of physical advantages and mineral wealth, with only a strip of inhospitable sea-board, held her own against all the forces of Spain, and has become one of the greatest commercial centres of Europe. It is only blindness itself which cannot see that it is owing to moral, rather than to physical, causes that nations rise and fall. The readers of Gibbon's immortal work* well know that it was owing to the decay of those moral qualities which raised ancient Rome to be the mistress of the world, that she fell from her high estate; and this became accentuated when Christianity, which ought to have been a regenerating force, shared in the common debasement of public spirit and morals.

So long as England remains true to the principles which have made her great she need fear no foe. If her coal-mines are being exhausted, the worst that can happen to her is to revert to the character which Virgil gives of ancient Italy:—" Terra potens armis atque ubere glebæ." To maintain the command of the sea is our highest policy; a policy which we have inherited from the days of Queen Elizabeth, and which is well expressed by Lord Bacon when he says:—" Surely, at this day with us in Europe, the

---

* 'The Decline and Fall of the Roman Empire,' vols. vii., viii, and ix.

vantage of strength at sea (which is one of the principal dowries of this kingdom of Great Britain) is great; both because most of the kingdoms of Europe are not merely* inland, but girt with the sea most part of their compass, and because the wealth of both Indies seems, in great part, but an accessory to the command of the seas." † What was true in Lord Bacon's time is true to-day. We must maintain our navy in its full strength. This being so, it may be replied that, should our coal be diminished, it will be impossible for us to maintain a position which appears to be so largely dependent on the abundant supply of this mineral fuel.

But we must recollect that other countries of Europe which are our rivals, may they never be our foes! are also drawing heavily upon their own coal supplies. It would be interesting to know to what extent the coal beds of France, Belgium, and Germany are being exhausted by mining. Whether any estimates have been made of the coal-resources of these countries is unknown to us; but to a greater or less extent the same process of exhaustion which is going on in Great Britain is also in progress in European states.‡ Whatever falling off may arise in arts and manufactures in this country will also take place in Continental States; nor, as the late Pro-

* Completely.
† *Essays*, with Whateley's Annotations, No. xxix.
‡ See Appendix III.

fessor Jevons has shown, when controverting the views of the writer as held many years ago, but now abandoned, can the manufactures of one country be sustained by imports of coal from foreign parts.* The same writer has examined the question of the possible substitutes for coal, such as the power derived from the tides; electricity, which is really not a source of, but only a distributing agent for, power; petroleum and other suggested substitutes; and he comes to the conclusion that there is no possible substitute for coal; except on the principle that "half a loaf is better than no bread." All others would fall immeasurably short of a substance so easily portable and containing in itself such a vast amount of latent power. "All things considered," he says, "it is not reasonable to suppose or expect that the power of coal will ever be superseded by anything better," or, as he might have said, " as good." †

Petroleum is the favourite substance suggested as a substitute. But the quantity of this material derived from the distillation of oil-shale in Scotland is but trifling compared with the production of coal in that country alone; and, from foreign countries the total import into Great Britain, and used in this country, only amounted to 634,303 ‡ tons in 1895, and

---

* 'The Coal-question,' chap. xii.   † *Ibid.*, chap. vii. p. 142.
‡ Or 177,146,628 gallons, of which 1,761,246 gallons were afterwards exported; Statistical Abstract for the U.K., 1896. One ton of petroleum equals 276·5 gallons at sp. gr. 0·81.

even if we credit petroleum with three times the effective power of coal per ton, the proportion imported will only be one-hundredth of that due to the coal raised from British mines. Nor is petroleum any more than coal an inexhaustible product of nature. Many of the old wells of America have already been drained of their supplies, and this process will continue till the great underground reservoirs of liquid fuel with which nature has so remarkably endowed the American continent, are drained of their contents.

Thus we have seen that while our coal-resources are being rapidly reduced, there is no known substitute for those vast stores of mineral fuel with which these islands have been so lavishly endowed by nature. It is for statesmen to consider whether in the near future some restrictive impost should not be put upon the export of coal to foreign countries not for the use of British demands. Even were this desirable, there would be great difficulty in distinguishing foreign from home use except where there was direct shipment to foreign ports. The remedy would be scarcely worth the venture, and I do not advocate its adoption.

To us of this generation the discussion of the question regarding the future of these islands upon the approach to exhaustion of our coal-supplies is only one of academical interest. Still, we cannot but foresee that when this period approaches, a vast change in the social habits of the people must ensue. The relations of manufactures to agriculture which were prevalent (shall we say) in the days of George III. may be again repeated; but with modifications which it is impossible to foresee.

Meanwhile our duty is clear ; namely, to husband our resources. Waste should before all things be avoided both in the extraction of the precious mineral from its native bed, and in its subsequent use—whether in the furnace, the factory, or the residence. There is reason to believe that much progress has been made, in recent years, in this direction, but doubtless there is still room for further improvement in the economical use of coal.

APPENDIX I.

OUTPUT OF COAL FROM THE COAL-FIELDS OF THE UNITED KINGDOM SINCE 1870.[*]

Year.	Tons.
1870	110,431,192
1871	117,352,028
1872	123,497,316
1873	128,680,131
1874	126,590,108
1875	133,306,485
1876	134,125,166
1877	134,179,968
1878	132,612,063
1879	133,720,393
1880	146,969,409
1881	154,184,300
1882	156,499,977
1883	163,737,327
1884	160,757,779
1885	159,351,418
1886	157,518,482
1887	162,119,812
1888	169,935,219
1889	176,916,724
1890	181,614,288
1891	185,479,126
1892	181,786,871
1893	164,325,795
1894	188,277,525
1895	189,661,362
1896	195,361,260

[*] From the 'Mineral Statistics, U.K. for 1895.' (1896).

APPENDIX II.

(Communicated by the Home Office.)

PRODUCTION OF COAL IN THE UNITED KINGDOM DURING THE YEAR 1896, AS FURNISHED TO THE INSPECTORS OF MINES.

ENGLAND.

County.	Tons.
Cheshire	775,405
Cumberland	1,931,771
Derbyshire	11,774,957
Durham, North	9,592,201
,, South	23,170,338
Gloucestershire (Bristol District)	337,254
,, (Forest of Dean)	896,679
Lancashire, North and East	10,172,792
,, West	12,438,223
Leicestershire	1,517,217
Monmouthshire	8,841,379
Northumberland	9,027,752
Nottinghamshire	6,623,529
Shropshire	720,130
Somersetshire	871,373
Staffordshire, North	4,788,608
,, South	8,277,527
Warwickshire	2,430,770
Westmoreland	1,258
Worcestershire	852,743
Yorkshire, West Riding	23,939,659
,, North Riding	3,829
Total	138,985,394

WALES.

County.	Tons.
Breconshire	272,605
Carmarthenshire	1,042,668
Denbighshire	2,233,365
Flintshire	659,674
Glamorganshire	23,630,411
Pembrokeshire	80,858
Total	27,919,581

SCOTLAND.

	Tons.
Argyll and Dumfries	127,122
Ayrshire	3,565,729
Clackmannan	329,580
Dumfries (included with Argyll)	..
Dumbarton	494,861
Edinburgh	1,096,956
Fife	3,633,455
Haddington	352,920
Kinross, Peebles, and Sutherland	5,619
Lanark, East	8,413,544
,, West	7,391,757
Linlithgow	882,961
Peebles (included with Kinross)	..
Renfrew	46,057
Stirling, East	1,211,953
,, West	774,186
Sutherland (included with Kinross)	..
Total	28,326,700

SUMMARY.

Country.	Tons.
England	138,985,394
Wales	27,919,581
Scotland	28,326,700
Ireland	129,585
Total for United Kingdom	195,361,260

APPENDIX III.

SINCE the passage in page 143 was in type, I received information through my friend Sir Charles Oppenheimer, H.B.M. Consul-General at Frankfort, that an inquiry into the coal-resources of some of the Continental States had been made, and the results published in a short treatise by Geh. Bergrath R. Nasse in 1893.* This was interesting tidings, as showing that Continental States had been turning their attention, like ourselves, to the important question—how long their supplies of coal were destined to last; especially in view of the great increase in production which has taken place in recent years.† I now proceed to give the reader a brief *résumé* of Herr Nasse's treatise, referring to the treatise itself for fuller details.

The author commences by the consideration of similar questions to those which have occupied ourselves, regarding the possible depths of coal-mining depending on temperature, quality and thickness of the seams, and arrives at very similar conclusions.

With regard to increase of underground temperature he states that experience has shown that effective mining work cannot be carried on under a higher temperature than 40° Cent. (104° Fahr.), in moist air, and 50° Cent. (122° Fahr.) in very dry air; and estimating for the rate of increase in descending, he considers that mining will become impossible at more than 900 metres (in round numbers 3000 feet) in damp, and 1200 metres (4000 feet) in dry air.‡ In the Ste. Henriette des Produits mine in Belgium, mining is carried on with much difficulty, owing to the high temperature, at a depth of 3900 feet from the surface at present. The author does not apprehend much difficulty in working the seams, owing

* 'Die Kohlenvorräthe der Europäischen Staaten,' Berlin, 1893.
† See p. 133 *et seq.*
‡ It will be observed that this is the limit adopted in this work, see p. 4.

to the pressure of superincumbent strata at great depths; but the question of the least thickness of the workable seams of coal is one on which he expresses a very decided opinion. Given a seam of good quality, with good roof and floor, wages moderate, and price sufficient to give a fair profit, he does not think that seams under two feet in thickness will be worked at considerable depths; and as an illustration of his view he states that it has been found in Belgium that seams of 40 centimetres (about 1¼ foot), and 60 centimetres (about 2 feet) in the Saar and Rhur districts have been found not worth working.* The amount taken as an average for loss in working coal-mines is placed at 23 per cent., but this quantity is exclusive of the amount which has to be left untouched under large buildings, canals and towns.

The inquiry into the coal-resources of Germany was commenced as far back as 1858 by Herr von Dechen, and published in a statistical work at the time.† Since then many years have elapsed, while the production of coal has enormously increased in all the German coal-basins, thus calling for newer and more reliable estimates.

In the summer of 1890, the Prussian Inspector of Mines (Oberbergämter) received from Freiherrn von Verlepsch the commission to set on foot inquiries regarding the extent and resources of the different coal-basins of the German States, with other details regarding the area of workings, and quantities of coal at various depths down to 1000 metres and over. The results have since been published, and almost simultaneously therewith were issued those of the Kingdom of Saxony; so that, as far as the more important coal-districts in Germany are concerned, the answer as to the duration of the coal-supplies can now be freshly attempted. This could be easily given were the annual production to remain constant, but it is otherwise with a production which has been annually increasing. The bearing of this production on the resources is then discussed for each State, and supplemented by tables

---

* This is confirmatory of the adoption of a 2-feet limit of thickness in estimating the resources of the British coal-fields, which has been followed in this work, see p. 3.

† 'Statistik des zollvereinten und nördlichen Deutschlands'

of output—which need not detain us here—as those of more recent date have already been given.* The following is the general result of the resources of coal (steinkohle) in Germany:—

District.	Tons.
Ruhr	50,000,000,000
Saar	10,400,000,000
Aachen	1,800,000,000
Upper Silesia	45,000,000,000
Lower „	1,000,000,000
Kingdom of Saxony	400,000,000
Remaining small districts	400,000,000
Total	109,000,000,000

In brown coal the amount is 3000 millions of tons. The whole of the above is contained within 1000 metres in depth from the surface.

As regards France, M. A. de Lapparent estimated that for the output of 1890, there was sufficient coal to last for 700 or 800 years, which would represent from 17 to 19 milliard tons then remaining unexhausted. For Belgium no estimate of resources has yet been made; nor is this surprising, when we consider the remarkably contorted, faulted, and folded condition in which the coal-formation of that country has been left by nature.

APPENDIX IV.

THE total make of British pig-iron for 1896 was 8,563,209 tons; an increase of 667,534 tons on the output of the previous year, and the largest yet reached in this country, yet falling short of the production in the United States in 1890 and 1895, when the make reached about 9 million tons.—Art. 'British Iron and Steel Industries,' *Times*, 14th April.

* *Ante*, pp. 132-4.

INDEX.

ADMIRALTY dockyards, 16
Air-currents in coal-mines, 123, 126
America; United States, naval construction of, 13
Anglia, East, absence of coal under, 39
Anthracite, composition of, 9
Argyllshire coal-field, 81
Armstrong, Lord, quoted, 109
Atkinson, Mr. W. N., quoted, 54, 126
Atherstone, absence of coal north of, 101
Atmosphere, effect of humidity or dryness in coal-mines, 126
Austria-Hungary, coal-production in 1893, 134
Ayrshire coal-field, 77

BAGWORTH colliery, 97
Beech, Mr. Noel T., quoted, 53
Belfast, ship-building in, 15
Belgium, coal-production in 1894, 134
Bertrand, M. Marcel, on coal under south of England, 85
Binns, Mr. George J., quoted, 137
Borings for coal in the Midlands, 28, 97
— — — — Suffolk, &c., 95
Brady, Mr. F., on "The Kent coal-field," 85
Bristol and Somerset coal-field, 56
Burnley coal-basin, 50

"CALCIFEROUS series" of Scotland, 73
Cambro-Silurian rocks under the east of England, 95
Canobie coal-basin, 78
Canada, value of coal in, 139
Cape of Good Hope, output of coal in 1894, 137
Census of population, 1895, 7
China, coal in, 137
Canada, coal-production in 1893 and 1894, 136
Canobie coal-field, 48
Cannock Chase, coal at, 32
Cantrill, Mr. T. C., quoted, 55
Cardiff as a shipping port, 64
Clackmannan coal-field, 76
Clyde basin, coal-field of, 74
Coal Commission, report, 3, 25, &c.
Coal-fields of—
  Australia, 136
  Austria-Hungary, 134, 139
  Ayrshire, 77
  Belgium, 134, 138, 139
  Bristol, 56
  Burnley, 50
  Canobie, 48
  Cape of Good Hope, 137
  Cheshire, 50, 100, 102, 104, 129
  Clackmannan, 76
  Clyde basin, 73, 74
  Cumberland, 48
  Coalbrook Dale, 53, 130
  Denbighshire, 69, 99, 102, 104
  Derbyshire, 41, 90, 100

Coal-fields of—
  Durham and Northumberland, 45, 90
  Fifeshire, 76
  Flintshire, 70
  Forest of Dean, 60, 129
  Forest of Wyre, 33, 55
  France, 134, 139
  Haddington, 75
  India, British, 136, 139
  Ireland, 91
  Japan, 134
  Lancashire, 50, 102, 104, 129
  Leicestershire, 34, 96, 101, 104, 129
  Lesmahago, 78
  Mid-Lothian, 75
  Natal, 137
  New South Wales, 137, 139
  New Zealand, 137, 139
  Notts, Derbyshire and Yorkshire, 41, 90, 100
  Queensland, 137
  Shropshire, 53
  South Wales, 62
  Spain, 134, 139
  Staffordshire, North, 29, 101, 129
  Staffordshire, South, 32, 96, 101, 104, 129
  Tasmania, 137
  Tyrone, 25, 91
  United States of America, 135, 139
  Victoria, 137
  Wales, South, 62, 129
  — North, 68, 129
  Warwickshire, 37, 90, 96, 100, 104
  Yorkshire, 41, 100, 129
Coal-fields, classification of, 26
— Foreign, 10, 132
Coaling stations, 9
Coal, low price of, 19
— output of, in 1895, 106

Coal, output of, in 1896, Appendix II.
— resources of United Kingdom, total estimates of, 105
— — —Continental States, Appendix III.
— south of the Thames, 85
Concealed coal-areas, 92
Cooke, Mr. C. J. Bowen, quoted, 11
Craven colliery, 100
Cunard Company, 16
Cumberland coal-field, 48

DAWKINS, Prof. Boyd, on coal under Kent, 85
Denbighshire coal-field, 69
Depth of coal-mining, limit of, 4
— — — average, 22
— — coal-seams, 5, 23, 51, 83, 129
— — collieries, South Wales, 68
— — — North Wales, 69
— — — Lancashire, 51
— — — Derbyshire, 110
— — — Leicestershire, 110
— — — Nottinghamshire, 110
De Rance, Mr. C. E., quoted, 50
Dickinson, Mr. J., quoted, 51, 52, 69
Dover, coal proved at, 85, 96
Dukinfield colliery, experiments on temperature at, 112
Dumfries-shire coal-basins, 78
Durham coal-field, 45

ECCLES, Lancashire, 100
Eden, Vale of, coal under, 100, 103, 104
Edinburghshire coal-basin, 75
Elliot, the late Sir George, quoted, 46
Etheridge, Mr. R., quoted, 57, 95
Expansion of coal-mining, 6
Export of coal, 8, 51, 67, 82
— — iron, 12

INDEX.

FIFESHIRE coal-field, 76
Flintshire coal-field, 70
Forth, Firth of, coal under the, 80
Forster, Mr. T. E., quoted, 46, 48
Foster, Mr. C. Le Neve, quoted, 21, 28
France, coal-production in 1894, 134

GEDDES, Mr. John, quoted, 75, 77, 79
Geikie, Sir A., quoted, 76
Germany, coal-production in 1894, 133
Glasgow coal-field, 74

HAMSTEAD Colliery, 32
Hartley, Mr. John, quoted, 33, 55
Hedley, Mr. J. L., quoted, 46
Hetton colliery, effect of ventilation in, 126
Hopkinson, Mr. J., quoted, 95
Howell, Mr. H. H., quoted, 76
Hughes, Mr. H. W., quoted, 33, 40
Hunt, late Mr. Robert, quoted, 7, 17
Hurlet coal-seam, 75

INDIA, British, coal-production of, 136
Ireland, coal-resources of, 25, 91
Iron-ores, 10, 11
Ironstone of Scotland, 74, 83
Iron-trade of Glasgow, 82
Italy, lignite and coal-production 1893, 134

JAPAN, coal-production in 1893, 135
Jevons, the late Prof., quoted, 2, 109, 143

Jones, Mr. Daniel, quoted, 33, 53, 55
Jordan, Mr. J. B., 6, 61

KENT, coal under, 85
Knowles, Mr. John, quoted, 126

LANCASHIRE coal-field, 50, 100
Lapworth, Professor, quoted, 40, 98
Leicestershire coal-field, 34
Lesmahago coal-field, 78
Lilleshall colliery, 54

MANUFACTURERS, British, 10
Marston, Cheshire, boring at, 50
Meacham, Mr. F. G., quoted, 33
Mendip Hills, 57, 87
Midland coal-fields, 28, 29
"Mineral Statistics of Great Britain," 3, 18, 24
Mining, limit of deep, 107, 109
Mining under the sea, 45, 46, 47, 48
—— Firth of Forth, 80
Mold, Flintshire, oil-works at, 71
"Mountain mines" of Lancashire, 51

NATAL, output of coal in 1894, 137
Navy, the Royal, 8
Newcastle-on-Tyne, 131
Newport, Monmouthshire, 64
New South Wales, coal-fields, 137
—— —— output of coal, 1894, 137
—— —— value of coal at the pit-mouth, 139
New Zealand, output of coal in 1894, 137
—— value of coal in, 139
Nottinghamshire coal-field, 41
— future of mining in, 43

OUTPUT of coal, United Kingdom, from 1870 to 1896, Appendix I.
— — — arranged according to counties for 1896, Appendix II.
— — — in the coal-fields, United Kingdom, for the year 1895, 106

PETROLEUM, consumption of, in Great Britain, 1895, 144
Pig-iron, 11, 12
Peninsular and Oriental Company, 16
Pennant rock, 57, 65
Percentage of coal consumed in foreign countries, 140
Permian strata pierced by coal-shafts, 37, 41, 42, 45, 50, 52, 92
Pig-iron, British, production of, in 1895, 11
— — — — — 1896, Appendix IV.
Population, rate of increase, 7
— proportion of coal consumed per head, 17
Pressure, effect of, in mines, 128
Prestwich, the late Sir J., quoted, 53, 56, 59, 85, 87
Production of coal from 1879 to 1883, 20
Progressive and retrogressive mining districts, 129, 130

QUEENSLAND, output of coal in 1894, 137

RAILWAY extension in the future, 12
Ramsay, the late Sir A. C., on coal below the Trias and Permian, 93, 94, 99, 101, 103
Resources, summary of, in visible coal-fields, 90

Resources, summary of, in concealed coal-areas, 99, 100
Retrogressive coal-areas, 130
Revised estimates of coal-resources (concealed), 103
— — — — in the visible and concealed coal-fields, within a depth of 4000 feet, at the close of this century, 105
Ritchie, Mr. C. T., quoted, 12
Robson, Mr. J. T., quoted, 67
"Roman Camp Limestone," 75
Rose Bridge colliery, experiments at, 4, 115
Russian Empire, coal-production of (1893), 133

SANDWEEL Park colliery, 32
Sanquahar coal-basin, 78
Scarle, boring at, 42
Scott, Mr. M. W. T., quoted, 53
Scottish coal-fields, 73
Seasons; influence on temperature in mines, 125
Ship-building in the United Kingdom, 15, 16, 17
Shire Oak colliery, 42
Sliding scale, advantages of, 19
South Carr, boring at, 41
Spain, coal-production in 1894, 134
Spurs of Lower Silurian and Cambrian rocks in the Midlands, 35
Staffordshire, North, coal-field, 29, 31
— South, coal-field, 32
Stationary coal-areas, 130
Steam-coal, 8, 86
— of South Wales, 9, 65
Steel, use of, for railways, 10
— — — — ships, 13
Stokes, Mr. A. H., quoted, 33, 100, 110
Strikes in trade, effects of, 19
Swansea, South Wales, 64

INDEX.

Sweden, lignite-production in 1894, 133
Sydney Harbour, coal under, 137

TASMANIA, output of coal in 1894, 137
Temperature of deep mines, 111
— rate of increase of, 115, 117, 118
— table showing rate of increase of, at various depths, 121
Triassic strata pierced by coal-shafts, 50, 52, 92

UNITED States of America, coal-production in 1893-4, 135
— — — iron-production, Appendix IV.

VALUE of coal at pit's mouth in various countries, 139

Ventilation of coal-mines, effect of, 122
Victoria, output of coal in 1894, 137
Vivian and Clark's, Messrs., estimates of South Wales basins, 66, 67
Volcanic rocks of Scotland, 77

WALES, North, coal-fields, 68
— South, coal-basin, 62, 129
— intersecting valleys, 64
Warwickshire coal-field, 37
— resources of, 38
Whitaker, Mr. W., on coal under the eastern counties, 95
Wirral Promontory, coal under, 100, 103, 104
Wood, Mr. Lindsay, quoted, 126
Woodhouse, the late Mr. J. T., 36, 38, 44
Wyken Colliery, 37, 38, 97

www.ingramcontent.com/pod-product-compliance
Lightning Source LLC
Chambersburg PA
CBHW030301170426
43202CB00009B/827